THE SUBJECT LIAISON'S
SURVIVAL GUIDE
TO TECHNICAL SERVICES

The Subject Liaison's Survival Guide to Technical Services

KRISTA SCHMIDT

TIM CARSTENS

AN IMPRINT OF THE AMERICAN LIBRARY ASSOCIATION

CHICAGO   2017

KRISTA SCHMIDT has worked in libraries for fifteen years and was the first dedicated subject liaison hired by Hunter Library at Western Carolina University (WCU). She currently serves as the STEM liaison and maps librarian at WCU and has spent six years on the university library's collections advisory committee. Krista has a BA in biology from Illinois Wesleyan University and an MSLS from the University of North Carolina at Chapel Hill. She was named a 2013 Mover and Shaker by *Library Journal*.

TIM CARSTENS graduated from Colby College with a BA in philosophy/religion and received his MLS from Rutgers University. He was a monographic cataloger at North Carolina State University from 1984 until 1990 when he began working for Western Carolina University in Cullowhee, North Carolina. Tim has served as head of the Cataloging and Acquisitions Unit and the Content Organization and Management Department, and his responsibilities have included collection development, acquisitions, cataloging and metadata, serials, and electronic resources. Tim was appointed associate dean of Library Services at Hunter Library in 2014 before retiring in 2016.

© 2017 by the American Library Association

Extensive effort has gone into ensuring the reliability of the information in this book; however, the publisher makes no warranty, express or implied, with respect to the material contained herein.

ISBNs
978-0-8389-1502-8 (paper)
978-0-8389-1532-5 (PDF)
978-0-8389-1533-2 (ePub)
978-0-8389-1534-9 (Kindle)

Library of Congress Cataloging in Publication Control Number: 2016040888

Cover design by T.J. Johnson. Text design in the Chaparral, Gotham, and Bell Gothic typefaces.

♾ This paper meets the requirements of ANSI/NISO Z39.48-1992 (Permanence of Paper).

Printed in the United States of America

21 20 19 18 17   5 4 3 2 1

For all current and future subject liaisons
and their technical services colleagues.
—KS and TC

Io my parents, the ultimate cheerleaders.
And to the SchmConnells—Seán, Aeryn, and Miles.
You make me happy when skies are gray.
—KS

This book is also dedicated to the memory
of former colleague Edward Cohen,
past head of Reference at Western Carolina University.
—TC

Contents

7 | **Collection Maintenance** *67*

Acknowledgments

We would like to acknowledge all those who assisted in the development of this idea and the creation of this book. To all our colleagues, both past and present, but especially our colleagues who read, advised, and supplied their expertise: Elizabeth Marcus, Cara Barker, Kristin Calvert, Dana Wood, Katy Ginanni, and Tina Adams. We thank you so much; we couldn't have done it without you. We also express our deepest appreciation to Heidi Buchanan, who, in addition to reading our manuscript, set us on this path one warm night in Charleston by remarking, "You could turn this into a book, you know." We also must recognize super-librarian Sarah Steiner who opened the door to ALA Editions for us. Thank you, Sarah!

Introduction

This guide is intended to help subject liaisons, particularly those new to the profession, better understand the complexities of technical services as they relate to collection development. This idea originated from a single, long-ago presentation, experiences working together on a joint technical services/subject liaison collections committee, and our own conversations and experiences with veteran and new subject liaisons. We found that there was not only a need for liaisons to understand some of the nitty-gritty aspects of technical services as they relate to the collections aspects of a liaison's job but also no easy or practical way to cover all that ground when someone is brand new. We also found that although there is plenty of literature about technical services such as cataloging or acquisitions, the primary audience is not subject liaisons. And although much has been written about the collection responsibilities of a liaison, there is a dearth of in-depth information about technical services as it relates to liaisons and their collection responsibilities. This short volume is our attempt to address this lack of information and to provide subject liaisons with a starting point as they begin to build their understanding of technical services.

At this point, it behooves us to define what we mean when we refer to *technical services* and *subject liaisons* because these can be defined, named, and organized differently depending on the library. A *liaison* is an academic librarian who has three primary responsibilities: reference/research assistance, library instruction, and collection development. These responsibilities are subject-specific, meaning that the liaison provides these services to meet the needs of disciplines such as engineering, psychology, theater, education, and the like. Many liaisons have responsibilities in more than one discipline or subject area. *Technical services,* in this book, is a catchall term we use to refer to the units or departments responsible for collection development and maintenance, acquisitions, processing, and cataloging.

ORGANIZATION

In order to give subject liaisons a starting point for developing a more robust understanding of technical services, we organized our chapters into what we considered a logical flow that mostly follows the process of acquiring resources: developing the collection, budgeting, submitting orders, acquisitions ordering, receiving and processing, cataloging, and maintaining the collection. Each chapter is divided further into the main points of interest for the overarching chapter theme. These subdivisions provide a brief explanation about the importance of the topic for liaisons and some context for the topic. These discussions are followed by lengthy lists of questions we've titled "Questions You Should Be Asking." These questions are meant to be the true guide for liaisons by pointing them toward considerations of which they were unaware and by providing starting points for conversations with technical services colleagues. Liaisons shouldn't feel constrained to sit down with technical services staff and ask all the questions at once; in fact, we don't recommend that approach. Rather, these questions should be used to guide *ongoing* conversations and learning. Many of these questions will be excellent starting points for these ongoing conversations, but we also expect that some questions may be more useful after a liaison has gained a little experience and begun working in earnest with technical services colleagues.

One final note on organization: at the end of the book, readers will find a glossary of the jargon and technical terms we've used. We've tried to keep definitions straightforward and free of too many details. Some of these terms may not have a standard use across libraries, so keep in mind that the definitions we provide are within the context of this book.

EXCLUSIONS AND CAVEATS

Before you move on to the heady reading beyond this introduction, we would like to address a few exclusions and caveats. First, please be aware that this book is not comprehensive. It does not cover every eventuality or every situation, nor is it meant to. There was simply no way for us to include everything in technical services that may be important to a liaison, so we opted to include what we thought was most likely to be commonly experienced. You may also notice, if you happen to be a technical services colleague reading this guide, that some details are not quite as precise as might be expected were you discussing the same topic with your technical services colleagues. This is a result of writing for an audience who needs details but not minutiae.

We also readily acknowledge that what we have included does not speak to every situation or environment. We don't assume that every library is the same or like our own institution; there are numerous ways to organize a library and its workflows. Likewise, individuals, even with the same job title, may have different roles, responsibilities, or levels of authority depending on the library in which they work. This book does not attempt to discuss the myriad ways in which libraries, liaisons, and technical services units can operate. We wrote this book with the premise that every library is in some way unique and that the only way that you can find out about your particular situation is to talk with the librarians and staff in your library. Just as your library may not refer to subject liaisons by that particular moniker or the term *technical services* might not be in use at all in your institution, there may be situations we address in this book that don't occur in your library. Or perhaps these aspects in your library are similar to what we address but not exactly the same. Our questions are meant to be thought-provoking and conversation starters; we aren't expecting them to be the end-all-be-all to the dialogue you establish with technical services and neither should you. We hope that you use them or rework them, if needed, to address your particular situation.

Finally, missing from this book is a philosophical examination of technical services as it relates to liaisons. How should I perform collection development? What is the importance of cataloging for patrons? What are the best statistics to use for decision making? Though there is a lot of value in addressing those questions, we have chosen to steer away from them because other sources have addressed those questions more robustly and because the point of a book on the practicalities of technical services would be lost. Instead, we hope we have included some questions that help you obtain the information you decide you need once you've considered these weighty topics.

We trust that the conversations inspired by these questions will help you understand how technical services really works in your library and that they help you as you develop into an experienced and effective liaison. We also hope that as you have these conversations, you'll see that much of collection development is a team effort and that building your understanding of these mechanics can help you navigate these processes effectively.

1
Collection Development

ollection development may be *the* part of technical services in which most liaisons expect to be involved. In this book and in the workaday world, too, *collection development* is a broad, catchall phrase that applies to everything from the organizational unit and the individual(s) responsible for collections to the concepts, policies, and processes related to developing, selecting, and maintaining collections.

In this chapter, our focus is on the unit responsible for collection development in your library. We recognize that libraries may use different names or locate this unit in different places in the organizational hierarchy; in this book, when we use the term *collection development*, we refer to the unit whose primary responsibilities pertain to the development of the library's collections or resources, regardless of actual official title or organizational placement. Rather than focusing on the theoretical aspects of collection development or explaining best practices on how to develop collections, this chapter primarily addresses the functional parts of the collection development department that we think affect the liaison most: understanding the departmental structure and associated liaison roles, communication to and from the department, the official collection development policy, and data or information that the department can provide.

STRUCTURE

Because collection development is a main responsibility for subject liaisons, we think it is imperative to understand exactly who is involved in collection development activities and oversight within the library. Understanding this structure is directly related to who has authority and ultimate responsibility for performing collection development activities. You will find that different individuals have various levels of responsibility and that this arrangement varies widely by institution. Understanding structure helps you, as a liaison, understand exactly what your role is. Institutionally, a liaison's role can range from merely suggesting that the library purchase resources to making recommendations for purchase that are routinely accepted to actually having final authority over selection decisions. There are almost endless ways to organize a collection development department and delegate responsibilities. If you talk to liaisons who work in other institutions, you may find that in their library just one person coordinates all collection development activities while in other libraries, these responsibilities are divided among several people based on resource type (serials, electronic resources, one-time purchases, etc.). You may also find that some libraries use a committee—in addition to the individuals in the collection development department—to perform certain types of selection and decision making, perhaps for very expensive purchases or any item that requires a subscription.

There also may be outside players such as teaching or research faculty who have a role within the overall collection development structure, though the formality and prominence of their roles will vary by institution size, by library mission, or by both. We realize that this is very likely to seem like a confusing puzzle at first (for Thing X, ask Tom; for Thing Y, notify Lorenzo; for Issue Z, you'll need to consult with the Committee on All Things Print—and don't forget to include faculty!). If your library provides collection development training, the people responsible for many of the bigger aspects will become clear quickly. If not, start with trying to find an organizational chart with job descriptions for collection development and go from there. Absolutely ask questions of your technical services and liaison colleagues as you suss out exactly who is responsible for what, keeping in mind that what is written on organizational charts can be different in day-to-day practice.

STRUCTURE
Questions You Should Be Asking

Collection Development Department

- What functions does the collection development department perform?
- How many people are in this department?
- Are there any subunits (e.g., units responsible for particular resource types or subject areas) within the collection development department? If so, what are they, and what are their functions?
- Who leads this department, and is this individual the main decision maker?
- What is the collection development department leader's responsibility regarding selection, withdrawal, and other collection development decisions?

Collection Development Committees

- What functions, if any, do collections committees play in collection development? What is their responsibility regarding selection, withdrawal, and other collection development decisions?

- How many committees are there, what do they do, and what are they named?
- To whom do these committees report?
- Do liaisons serve on these committees? If so, what are the terms and responsibilities of the service?
- Who is the final decision maker—the committee (by consensus or vote) or the individual(s) to whom the committee reports?

Faculty

- What is the role of teaching or research faculty, or both, in collection development, particularly regarding resource selection and withdrawal? Does their role vary (e.g., do research faculty have more influence than teaching faculty)?
- Is the role of faculty in collection development formally recognized and documented? If so, where is this documentation?
- If the faculty's role is more informal, though still expected, what are the areas in which they should be included?

COMMUNICATION

In this book, we talk a lot about the importance of understanding how communication flows in and among departments. Because collection development responsibilities may be spread widely throughout the library, getting a good handle on the manner in which formal and informal communication flows to and from the collection development department is critical for success—as well as for avoiding frustration. Find out what kinds of communication you can expect to receive from the collection development department—such as policy updates and changes, deadlines, and guidelines—and what information staff members expect you to convey to their department, to faculty, and to vendors.

One of the first things about which a liaison can ask is the communication structure: who is responsible for relaying information about collection development? Although it might seem obvious that the communication structure should reflect the structure of collection development in general, you may find that only one person is responsible for relaying certain types of information—for example, policy updates, structure changes, collections decisions. You may also find that both formal and informal communication channels exist, as is the case in most departments. Collection development documentation may outline these channels, but don't forget to talk to your established liaison colleagues. They can offer their opinions and experiences on what you can expect and on effective approaches for relaying information to the collection development department through both channels, as well as alerting you to any unwritten rules or expectations (yes, these often exist!).

Liaisons will also want to determine how collection development–related communication with faculty and other key constituencies works, particularly the roles and expectations of the liaison versus the roles and expectations of the responsible parties in collection development. Ask about expected communications or reports to these parties from you or the collection development department or both, as well as how you are expected to report information or feedback from external partners to collection development. Communication with external-to-the-library constituents is critical in times of budget cuts and collection reviews. Because those situations tend to be touchy, it's crucial for liaisons to understand to whom and how cut/review processes are to be communicated to external partners. Be sure you clarify what information, if any, will be released by collection development to the external audience and what information should be disseminated by the liaison. For example, you may find that you want to include more information or context, or both, for the cuts than the minimum required by the collection development department, or perhaps you want to tailor the wording of a policy change message to make it more department-specific. We also urge you to recognize that there are times when the collection development department expects liaisons to disseminate a unified message with little to no deviation from the prepared script.

Liaisons should also consider the question of how communication works with resource providers or vendors. You will probably receive many, many calls and e-mails from vendors. And there will be times when you will want to ask vendors for specific types of information, including title lists, coverage, subscription or purchase costs, and so forth. Obviously you cannot control when vendors contact you, but be sure to check with the collection development department staff about their expectations for your conversations with vendors. There also may be times when collection development wants to be the main point of contact or to initiate contact with vendors—for example, to negotiate price or set up trials. You might find that the reasons in your library include a desire to convey consistent information or the need for formal record keeping. This doesn't mean that you can't or shouldn't participate in conversations with vendors along with collection development; rather, you need to recognize and understand when it is better to let the collection development department lead.

COMMUNICATION
Questions You Should Be Asking

- Who is the primary point person for general communication coming from collection development? If those responsibilities are divided, how is overall communication managed?

- What kinds of formal departmental communications can I expect to receive? How frequently does collection development send out various communiqués?

- What kinds of information am I required to report to collection development and how often? Are there formal reports that collection development expects liaisons to complete, or is reporting a more informal process?

- How is communication to teaching or research faculty regarding collection development issues handled? Are liaisons the primary communicators of information, or is the collection development department the primary issuer?

- If the collection development department issues most faculty communication, when will I be expected to either participate or lead?

- If collection development has a discussion with a faculty member or another department, am I automatically included in the conversation even though I may not be expected to be an active participant? If not, how can I make sure I'm informed of discussions that include my subject areas?

- If I, as the liaison, lead most of the faculty communication, in what situations will the collection development department need to assist or lead?

- Under what circumstances does the message from collection development need to be unified and unchanged by liaisons? Can I indicate that this message is from the library as an entity and not from me as an individual? What is the best wording for that circumstance?

- In communication with faculty about collection development issues—changes to policies, cuts, reviews—how detailed should the information be? Do we have any baseline information we are expected to include? Are there any guidelines for specific situations?

- Does most vendor communication happen between liaison and vendor or between collection development and vendor?

- When I communicate with vendors, what kinds of information should I be passing along to the collection development department? Should I be including the collection development department in my communications? If so, every time? Also, what individuals within collection development should I be notifying?

- Under what circumstances should I ask collection development to obtain vendor information for me rather than ask for it myself?

- When collection development talks to vendors of interest to my subject areas, will department staff include me in discussions? If this inclusion is done case by case, in what kinds of conversations do liaisons usually participate?

POLICY

Almost all libraries have an established collection development policy that serves as guidance for both virtual and physical collections. Although the text might not be riveting, it's important to read and develop a solid understanding of your library's policies because they contain a lot of institutionally specific information that you'll need to know for decision making. Policies provide guidance by outlining criteria for selection and deselection, indicating collection levels arranged by subject or classification, and identifying and prioritizing the collection's primary audiences (undergraduates, graduates, research, etc.). Expect the policy to specify the scope and breadth of the collection as well as set clear boundaries in specific areas.

Reading the library's collection development policy should be one of the first things that a new liaison does. You'll need to ask your collection development colleagues where policy documentation can be found and when it was last updated. You should also find out who maintains the policy—a person or a group—and with whom you should consult if you have any questions regarding the policy. We also strongly urge you to seek out the history and rationale of the policy because that information can provide valuable context regarding policy decisions contained within the document.

As you become familiar with the policies guiding collection development, the scope of said policies is another important aspect to investigate. By *scope*, we mean what information the policy includes and what it doesn't. For example, are collection development processes (e.g., physical handling of gift items, reporting dates and deadlines, etc.) addressed in the policy document itself, or are they dealt with elsewhere, if at all? As you read the policy and talk to colleagues, you may find that forming a complete picture of the policy and how it works requires other documentation in addition to the policy itself. We encourage you to find out who is responsible for maintaining and disseminating that type of information and then availing yourself of it.

Collection development policies are meant to be flexible and adaptable, but they may also need modifying from time to time as the library's mission, community, and resources evolve. As with other policy aspects, determining the *who* and the *how* should be on a liaison's short list of things to do: who can ask for modifications, who approves changes, who actually updates the document with modifications, how often changes are made, and how often routine reviews are conducted. Familiarizing yourself with those *whos* and *hows* will help you navigate the change process more effectively. Don't be afraid to ask about the history of past modifications because the changes and the reasons for them may give you some context for how decisions are made or why certain policies still exist (even when they don't necessarily make sense to you).

POLICY
Questions You Should Be Asking

- Where can I find the library collection development policy? How up to date is the policy? Are past versions available for review?

- Who is responsible for maintaining the collection development policy?

- If the procedures related to collection development policy are not contained within that document, where can I find them? What other supporting policy documentation exists?

- What is the process for suggesting changes to the collection development policy? Can these suggestions be made at any time, or is there a formal schedule for review and revision?

- Who makes the final decision regarding suggested changes, revisions, or additions to the policy? If this is done by a group, rather than an individual, are liaisons represented?

- When do policy changes go into effect? Is there a specific date that all policy changes go into effect, or are they effective upon approval?

DATA AND INFORMATION

The collection development department is a veritable font of information for liaisons and is an essential partner for acquiring, producing, and interpreting collections data. Typical types of data compiled and issued by collection development generally include usage and other statistical data—such as turnaways, average age, and so on—or cost information, and even resource analysis (e.g., coverage overlap, etc.). Collection development employees are also likely to have collection evaluation tools and other resources at their fingertips. These tools, when used with statistical data, can help liaisons identify strengths, weaknesses, and gaps by subject area or compare their collections with those of peer institutions. We recommend liaisons ask about other user assessment data, including results of recent user surveys, focus groups, and the like, particularly if those assessment data are captured regularly.

The collection development department can be a valuable resource for non-data information, too. For new liaisons, collection development staff may be familiar with teaching and research faculty who are actively interested in the library's collections and may then provide introductions to these faculty. In addition to helping identify potential faculty partners, collection development staff should be able to direct liaisons toward the course catalog and other sources of information about the current curriculum in their disciplines, including new and proposed courses or programs. All this information can usefully inform the liaison's selection activities.

DATA AND INFORMATION
Questions You Should Be Asking

- What are the main types of data collected and disseminated by collection development to liaisons? Is this regularly scheduled, or do I need to request it as needed? What is the procedure for requesting such data?

- What other resources, if any, are available to me for collections analysis? How can I use these resources? Is training available?

- Does the library participate in collections-related assessment activities, such as patron surveys, focus groups, and the like? Does assessment occur regularly, and, if so, how is it scheduled? If not, what determines when assessment happens?

- How can I get access to assessment data?

- If I need help interpreting and evaluating data I receive from collection development, who can help me?

- Does collection development track changes in programming and curriculum? If so, does the department disseminate that information to liaisons or must it be requested?

- If collection development doesn't track changes in programming and curriculum, where can I get that information? Can I find information about proposed, new, and existing courses and programs in one place?

- How can the collection development department staff help me find out about faculty members who have been active participants in collection development (policy, selection, weeding) in the past?

- Can collection development also educate me about faculty who may have special issues or concerns about the collection or about library processes?

2
Budgets and Budgeting

We realize it's tempting to ignore budget issues and just focus on spending what you are allocated. However, liaisons are well served to learn as much as possible about how budgets are determined and structured because understanding the overall budget situation allows you, as a liaison, to operate strategically. The projects you might realistically hope to accomplish, what requests from faculty and students might be supported, and day-to-day accomplishments are all dependent on the state of the budget. Also, understanding budgetary matters and terms enables liaisons to communicate more clearly and purposefully with collections and acquisitions colleagues. Such knowledge saves time in meetings when everyone understands what is meant by such terms as *allocation, encumbrance, expenditure,* or *reversion.* Finally, understanding the library budget and how it is allocated helps liaisons become truly effective advocates for the disciplines and academic departments that they serve. For example, let's say that you figure out that for your institution, student credit hours are heavily weighted in the allocation formula. This knowledge enables you to lobby in advance for more resource funds for a program that you know will be growing in the next few years or plan on how to absorb cuts when a department is shrinking. Developing an understanding of how collections budgets are put together at every level helps all liaisons understand the factors that affect funding.

UNDERSTANDING YOUR INSTITUTION'S AND LIBRARY'S FINANCIAL PICTURE

The first topic we're tackling in this chapter is learning about the bigger picture: the budget at the institutional and library levels. Don't worry, it's not necessary to learn *all* about how funding is structured in your institution. Instead, focus on the biggest of the big picture pieces: source of funds and who allocates the funds. If you understand these two aspects and their associated processes, the fundamental "Why are things this way?" question will be clearly answered.

Sources of Funds

Liaisons should begin by recognizing that there are many sources of institutional funds. These sources may include state allocations from tax revenues, tuition and fees, endowments, and the like. Depending on your institution, its type (public or private), and its reporting transparency, it may be easy to figure out from where the majority of the money that supports the university is derived. To start, we highly recommend looking at your institution's website to find the budget office, or its equivalent. A quick jaunt on the web shows that academic budget offices provide a plethora of information; some have the breakdown of sources in easy-to-read charts or reports, and most have an organizational chart—and budget policy information is found here, too.

BUDGET 101

The financial health of a university has many facets that are too complicated to explain here. However, there are a few things for liaisons to keep in mind when it comes to budgetary funds:

1. Full-time equivalent (FTE) enrollment affects overall institutional financial health.

2. Endowments, investments, and fund-raising play important supporting roles in the overall budget vision.

3. State-supported institutions often heavily depend on allocations from tax revenue.

All three of the preceding aspects can fluctuate from year to year and will not necessarily remain stable. And for state-supported institutions, state politics may weigh heavily in overall allocations from the state to the institution(s).

Liaisons will also want to find out about budget sources for the library as a whole and not just as they relate to the collections budget. Be aware that funds you see at the university level may not trickle down to an individual unit on campus; some are earmarked for other ventures, so the overall budget may not equate to what the library actually receives. Also, there may be sources of funding that don't appear in the beginning-of-the-year budget that the library receives but which can come to the library to supplement regularly allocated funds. These sources may include end-of-year (EOY) funds, endowments, grants, or fines and fees. These funds often come with special considerations. For example, end-of-year funds—one-time monies that become available at the end of the fiscal year as the university balances its books—require quick spending, and the amounts distributed vary widely over the years. This urgency and inconsistency make planning both crucial and difficult—though big windfalls make the planning worth it. Grants and endowments may require an application, which in itself often requires a significant amount of effort and might involve other offices on campus. For liaisons, this process

CUTS AND REVERSIONS

Many institutions, especially public ones, have to adjust budget expectations based on cuts or reversions, or both. At our institution, *cuts* are permanent reductions in the budget while *reversions* are one-time reductions whereby the unit or institution is required to "give back" funds to cover an unanticipated shortfall for a single year. Both of these processes have negative consequences for collections—liaisons should get to know the jargon surrounding any type of cut at their institution along with the regularity of these cuts and how the library plans for them.

results in less autonomy and more bureaucracy. Fines and fees from overdue or lost/damaged items may not even come back to the library.

Decision Making

It is probably not a surprise that decisions affecting the amount of the library's overall budget are made by administrative units external to the library and are determined by factors that don't necessarily fully consider the library or its needs. The yearly budget amount may be determined strictly by administrators, or a formalized, structured institutional process may be in place. We strongly urge liaisons to take the opportunity to participate in the budget process in any way possible, from serving on university or college budget committees to writing reports or gathering statistics that show a clear student or curricular need for resources. Remember that as a liaison, you've probably witnessed firsthand, by virtue of working directly with students and faculty on research and projects, how many and what kinds of resources are needed. This information is invaluable for the library administration as it seeks to demonstrate the need for additional funding.

UNDERSTANDING YOUR INSTITUTION'S AND LIBRARY'S FINANCIAL PICTURE

Questions You Should Be Asking

- What are the main sources of funds for the institution? Do these sources vary from year to year?
- Where can I find both overviews and detailed budget information for the institution? Will this information show me ongoing commitments (e.g., monies committed for long-term projects or ongoing expenses such as rent or utilities) that affect the overall budget?
- Does the institutional budget include known or anticipated cuts or reversions? If so, how much detail is included? If not, where can I find that information?
- Are previous years' institutional budgets archived? Is there a place to look at budgetary trends for the past five or ten years?
- What is the process at the institutional level for determining distribution of funds?
- Is a formal process in place for determining how budget funds are disbursed? Is the process public? Can I participate? When is a final determination made?
- Does my institution have, or is it planning, any large initiatives or mandatory obligations that might affect the availability of funds?
- What are the main funding sources for the library? Are these the same from year to year?
- Does the library provide detailed budget information itself? Where can I find this and what does it include?
- Does the library do any fund-raising to supplement its annual budget? If not, is there an outside group, such as Friends of the Library, that does?
- What happens to money from fees and fines? Does that money come back to the library?
- What sources of ad hoc funding (e.g., end-of-year funds, internal or external endowments, grants) might be available?

ALLOCATING FUNDS WITHIN THE LIBRARY

Now that the library has received funds from the institution, how is the library budget developed? With a few exceptions, the library itself chooses how to allocate funds, and all libraries have ongoing commitments (salaries, utilities, etc.) along with projects and initiatives that compete with collections for available funds. You should ask whether there is a formal process for determining budget allocations at the library level, and, if so, how that process works. If the process is informal or administrative in nature, understanding when and how the budget is decided and by whom is still worthwhile. As with the institutional budget, priorities might shift in any given year, so any "generally this is how the money is allocated" information you receive may change from one year to the next.

At some point, all the budgeting allocation from the institution down through the library is decided, and the final amount of the collections budget is determined. As a liaison, you will want to learn who controls the collections budget. Every library will have a different organizational structure that determines who controls what parts of the collections budget; one of the first tasks of any new liaison should be to determine that structure. You'll then know who to approach with budget questions. Whoever controls the budget is likely to divide the collections budget into two main funds: one-time purchases and continuing commitments.

One-time purchases are resources that the library buys outright and to which it has perpetual access until the library chooses to remove them. These resources include books, DVDs, music compact discs, and similar items. Continuing commitments are resources that require regular, ongoing payments to maintain access; these resources include journals and databases—really any resource purchased through subscription. The library is also likely to spend money on programs such as approval plans, standing orders, or demand-driven acquisitions (DDA) that require it to set aside funding in advance for future one-time purchases. These programs and, even more so, continuing resources consume large percentages of the collections

> ## CAN I MOVE MONEY FROM ONE FUND TYPE TO ANOTHER?
>
> It's not uncommon to receive a request from a faculty member or another patron to "stop spending money on *x* and spend it all on *y.*" For example, faculty patrons may ask to spend monograph money on journals. For the liaison, the question is this: "Can money be moved from one fund type to another upon request?" The answer is often, "It depends." It is crucial to talk to the budget decision makers about transferring funds and applicable policies before you start fielding this type of request.

budget. The high cost of these resources along with inflation often results in very tight budgets, year after year.

Once budget amounts are finalized for continuing and one-time purchases, further allotments may be made. Rules for allocation may vary depending on the type of information resources. Money is typically allocated to one-time funds through allocation formulas or historical precedents. Allocation formulas divide funds based on a predetermined set of criteria, which can be weighted. These factors may include student credit hours, number of majors, number of full-time faculty, circulation and use of materials, and so forth. When allocations are based on historical precedent, prior years' allocations are used as the starting point for determining current allocations. Allocations may then be adjusted in response to changes in a program, at the university, or in the scholarly publishing environment. In practice, the historical precedent and the allocation formula allow locally determined factors, environment, and professional judgment to influence the outcome. For liaisons, this means that the allocations received are almost always open to negotiation and adjustment. Still, to successfully argue for an adjustment, you must know first with whom to speak and then what criteria are used in decision making. For example, if the number of faculty in a program is one basis for making such decisions and you learn that a program you support

**BE A TEAM PLAYER
WHEN THERE ARE BUDGET CUTS**

This section of the book is all about ways liaisons can get more money to support programs. However, sometimes budget cuts loom, and you'll need to accept, as gracefully as possible, that you are likely to get less money and will need to make cuts. Keep in mind that cuts affect everyone; your colleagues will expect you to see the big picture—there are many competing needs for resources, and they cannot all be funded. When there are cuts, be prepared to absorb your fair share of the pain (as strategically as possible). Make your case for the essential resources but be prepared to sacrifice others.

has hired additional faculty, you will have strong cause for additional funding (yay you!).

In addition to these regular allocations, substantial amounts of money may be set aside for other one-time purposes, including purchasing reference works, very expensive one-time purchases, or resources for interdisciplinary topics that don't fit well within the traditional allocation structure. Liaisons should ask about these funds and how to request that these funds be used for specific purchase recommendations.

ALLOCATING FUNDS WITHIN THE LIBRARY
Questions You Should Be Asking

Budget and Funds

- Who decides how much money is allocated to the collections budget? Is this an individual or a group decision?
- What is the process for determining how much money comes to collections versus operations or other library budget areas?
- What current initiatives are under way that may reduce funding available for collections? Are there any future library initiatives or commitments that may further affect available funding?

- Who allocates the collections budget once it is finalized by the library? Is this a group or an individual?
- Beyond initial allocations, is there a person, group, or committee that regulates spending of collection development funds? If spending is controlled by a committee, who are the members? Do any liaisons serve on this committee? Does membership change or rotate?

Allocations and Allocation Formulas

- What kinds of allocation formulas, if any, are in use? What factors are considered in these formulas?
- Are the factors weighted? How were the weights determined? How much does changing the weights affect allocations?
- How often are formulas revised? What Is the process for requesting adjustments?
- Are allocation formulas used across the board, or are there different formulas for different materials (e.g., journals, books, DVDs, or similar items)?
- Is there any type of fund for which an allocation formula is not used?
- Is a process in place for making one-time adjustments (e.g., shifting from one fund to another for a single year)? Can such adjustments be done through the formula, or are simple flat amounts used?
- How much of the collections budget is committed up front to items such as journal or database subscriptions, approval plans, or DDA programs?
- How are funds allocated for interdisciplinary items? If two or more liaisons collect for an interdisciplinary subject, how is it decided how much each of us gets to spend? Is there a special fund, or do we each have to spend from our own funds?
- Are there ways to split costs across more than one fund? For example, if I want to split an expensive multidisciplinary encyclopedia set or an e-book package purchase with another liaison, is there a process for doing that?

- Are continuing resources assigned to disciplinary funds? If so, is this factored into overall disciplinary allocations?
- What is the process for requesting additional continuing resources or for making changes to the suite of continuing resources to which the library subscribes? How does this affect allocations?

Special Funds

- How can I find out what resource grants or end-of-year funds are available? Are end-of-year funds or grant monies factored into allocation formulas? If so, what is the process? If not, how do I request use of grant or EOY funds?
- Is there any regulation regarding what types of resources may be purchased with end-of-year monies?
- What special funds (e.g., leisure reading, reference resources), if any, are used in the library? Are these special funds strictly for one-time purchases, or can they be used for continuing resources? Do these special funds include funds for format updates or for replacements of damaged or lost items?
- What criteria determine how special funds may be used? Who regulates these criteria?
- What funds require a justification for using the allotment? Is the process formal or informal, and what are the details of that process? How often are requests from these funds considered?

Reversions and Cuts

- When reversions or cuts are impending, how are the cuts allocated among the funds? If I've already spent all my money and there's nothing left in my funds, what happens?
- How do cuts and reversions affect next year's allocation formula, if at all?
- Is there a way for me to prioritize my funds to minimize the impact of cuts on the most important subjects?

COMMUNICATION AND TIMING

Throughout this book, we tout communication as the key for developing understanding about all areas of collection development and acquisitions. As you learn about the budget, remember to ask about the frequency and timing of communication, particularly as it pertains to major budget issues or deadlines. Ask about how the institution communicates budget issues, too, as these definitely can affect how much you have to spend on collections. We discuss acquisitions communications, including budget issues, more thoroughly in chapter 3, "Submitting Orders," so we will be brief here: be prepared to ask the powers that be about formal and informal communication of budget issues, spending updates, and reports.

Every library has a budget schedule that includes both soft and hard deadlines; some deadlines will be externally imposed, and some will be internal. We recommend that liaisons spend time acclimating themselves to the budget cycle because it can have a big effect on the pace of your collection responsibilities. For example, it is not uncommon for spending to start at the beginning of the new fiscal year, even though the final library budget and allocations to collections funds may not be finalized until several months later. These situations can create both a lag and compression; you've held off placing too many orders because you didn't know the final amounts, and now you need to spend like crazy to meet spending benchmarks. We recommend that you find out right away whether you will need to adhere to a formalized, benchmarked time line or something more casual and find out how much flexibility—or not—there is on deadlines. As we mentioned, external forces may also affect deadlines and result in surprises such as end-of-year money, reversions, or even permanent cuts. We more thoroughly address timing issues in later chapters, but be aware that often the budget is the driving force behind major deadlines for all areas of acquisitions and collection development.

COMMUNICATION AND TIMING

Questions You Should Be Asking

- What is the process for providing liaisons with updates regarding the status of funds? Do updates or reports include amounts divided into statuses such as free, spent, and encumbered?

- How frequently are liaisons updated regarding funds? Do those updates reflect current activity, or is the information days or weeks old? Who provides these updates?

- Is it possible for liaisons to generate and view their own fund reports? If so, how? How up to date is the information in the tracking system (i.e., the integrated library system, or ILS)?

- When can liaisons begin spending the money in their funds? How does acquisitions notify liaisons that spending has commenced?

- What is the cutoff date when spending must cease? Is this a firm date? Does it change from year to year? What factors determine this date?

- What are the important dates for communication from the university regarding changes in the budget situation—for example, cuts, reversions, end-of-year money? Are these dates firm or general? How soon are liaisons notified if a change to the collections budget is anticipated?

- What policies regulate how spending can occur (e.g., for expensive items or unusual formats)? Are these regulations part of the collection development policy, or do they exist separately from that policy?

- How will I be notified when I get close to spending all allocated funds for a specific fund code? What happens if I overspend?

3
Submitting Orders

Submitting orders may be the most visible aspect of technical services in which liaisons are involved. After all, if a liaison chooses an item to purchase or recommend for subscription, then it follows that the submission of the item to acquisitions is also the responsibility of the liaison. This chapter focuses on *how* a liaison orders, a process that may seem simpler in theory than it is in practice because it frequently involves more than forwarding an e-mail or tearing a page out of a publisher's catalog. In fact, depending on the item and when it is submitted, the process can be quite complicated.

Before we discuss the main concepts related to submitting orders, we admit that we purposely skipped from budgeting to ordering without addressing *how* to select resources and build a collection. It isn't that we lack opinions on these topics; rather, we are omitting these because the philosophy and practicality of building a collection are book subjects of their own and are already thoroughly addressed in the library literature. However, we would be remiss if we left you with the idea that collection development can be separated from acquisitions. The acquisitions process is simply collection development executed.

ORGANIZATIONAL STRUCTURE

The first thing we recommend liaisons learn is the organizational structure of your acquisitions unit as it relates to submitting orders. Although some institutions may allow liaisons to order directly from vendors, others require mediated ordering, meaning the liaison submits the request to someone in acquisitions who then does the actual ordering of the item. In libraries with one person mediating orders, developing that understanding of the structure may be easy. For liaisons working in institutions with an acquisitions structure that splits ordering among multiple individuals, remembering who orders what can be much more challenging. As a liaison, you should also investigate the concept of mediated approval—that is, when items must go through an approval process before they can be ordered. This is usually the standard operating procedure for continuing resources; commitments to fund subscriptions generally are not based solely on liaison say-so. In addition to continuing resources, mediated approval may be required for very expensive, one-time purchases. Mediated approval requires discussion and then authorization for order by a collection development librarian or a collections committee or both. The mediated approval process can be lengthy and complex. You should be prepared for it to take longer and require more information than other types of submissions and understand that the organizational structure may take more effort to grasp.

So, how to remember processes that may seem convoluted? We have a two-part suggestion. First, we recommend that you determine how both formal and informal communications between acquisitions staff and liaisons are handled; some institutions have more rigid, hierarchical communication structures while others rely on more casual and fluid methods of communication. Contact the head of the unit or the supervisor but also seek information from your liaison colleagues so you can quickly develop an understanding of expectations and norms when it comes to seeking and passing along information in this role. Second, and maybe more obviously, talk to your colleagues in the acquisitions unit. You can look at a flowchart to get an organizational overview and that can be helpful, but often a flowchart doesn't include practical descriptions such as "Fred = Orders E-books" or "Daphne = Firm Orders, Print Items Only." Make an appointment directly with Fred and Daphne to ask what they do and what they don't do (we think the latter is as important as the former). If your library's structure is more formal and making appointments is more complex, start by making an appointment with the key contact in the unit and go from there.

Once you understand who handles what type of item and how information flows in and out of the department, you can route communications accordingly, and your interactions become more efficient and effective.

FACE-TO-FACE HAS ITS PLACE

Though so much is handled electronically in the workplace, we highly recommend sitting down face-to-face with your acquisitions colleagues for these initial meetings. Tone and nuance are pretty hard to convey electronically, despite the overwhelming presence of emojis and chat abbreviations in these types of conversations. And if you are new, you may not yet be familiar with the communication quirks of your colleagues. The warm-and-friendly-in-person colleague may write terse e-mails, while you may get a detailed message from someone who tends to be taciturn in person. Plus, we really believe that there is serendipity still to be found in a give-and-take conversation.

- How is acquisitions related to collection development? Are they separate and coexisting units or is acquisitions a subunit of collection development?

- Can a liaison order directly from a publisher or vendor? If so, are there any instances in which the liaison is not permitted to order an item directly—that is, acquisitions must submit the order to the vendor (mediated ordering)?

- For situations that require mediated ordering, is that process split or shared in the acquisitions department? If it is shared, among how many people?

- What types of orders require mediated approval? Who provides the final approval? Is it a committee or an individual? If it is a committee or group, does membership include liaisons? Does membership rotate?

- With whom should I communicate in acquisitions? Does the contact person vary by format type (e.g., print monograph, e-book, kit, game, DVD)? Does the contact person vary by fund used, such as one-time versus continuing monies?

- Who handles DDA?

- Who is responsible for approval plan setup? Who do I contact if I'm not satisfied with the approval plan or need to make changes?

- If I have fund issues or questions when I'm submitting orders, who do I contact? Is this contact person also responsible for processing and submitting my orders to vendors, or does someone else do that? Is there a different contact person for DDA or approval plan items?

INFORMATION AND PROCESSES

As a liaison, one of the fastest ways to realize your resource dreams is to include sufficient information for acquisitions. If there is a form or a vendor website to use, the fields there should indicate exactly what information is required. But if there is no form or website or if you have items that cannot be ordered that way, knowing the minimum information (e.g., title, author, edition, publisher, price) required to order an item is paramount for effectiveness and success. Why? Because providing this information from the outset means staff time is not needlessly spent tracking down information you should have had when you sent the acquisitions unit the initial request. Having the required information also helps ensure that an order does not languish in an "incomplete information" or "problem" pile. Liaisons should also be aware that additional information may be requested or even required in certain circumstances, such as when asking for an exception to established collection development policies or when requesting new continuing resource subscriptions. Be prepared to provide those additional pieces of information during the initial sub-mission process.

Submission processes can range in complexity within an institu-tion. Talking to acquisitions colleagues about both formal and infor-mal submission processes is useful because their answers can help you plan and be more efficient when submitting items for ordering. For example, understanding that all orders come with default set-tings (e.g., newest edition, specific platform, or paper-bound) may mean that notation to the contrary is necessary upon submission, or you may receive an unexpected item that you really do not want. For processes, liaisons should become familiar with not only how routine submissions work but also processes related to patron-driven acqui-sitions (PDA) or DDA, patron-initiated requests, and vendor-based approval plans.

INFORMATION AND PROCESSES
Questions You Should Be Asking

- For mediated approval submissions, what are the review parameters (e.g., duplication, price, format type)?

- What standard information needs to be included in submissions for monographs (e.g., author, title, standard number, publication date, edition statement, fund code)?

- What additional information is needed for specialty items such as out-of-print monographs or unusual format resources?

- What format for order submissions is allowed or preferred (e.g., electronic submissions, such as e-mail or through a vendor's online system; physical submissions, such as paper slips or pages from a publisher's catalog)?

- What kinds of resources require additional information or justification? Does it depend on the expense or the item type or both?

- What additional information is required for the purchase of resources that are not standard monographs? Are written justifications, detailed budgets, database trials, or other information expected?

- Are exceptions to the library's collection development policy ever allowed, and, if so, what is the process for deciding if they are possible?

- How should special instructions—such as "Notify Professor Matterhorn upon arrival" or "Rush"—be noted?

- Under what conditions should rush orders be submitted? What is the procedure for changing an already-submitted standard item to a rush item?

- How does special handling work—and how does that affect the overall process (e.g., spiral-bound notebooks should be sent to binding immediately)?

- How do standing orders work?

- How are replacement copies of physical items handled?

- How do DDA and approval plans affect liaison-submitted orders? How do you avoid duplication(s) in these situations?

- How are faculty-initiated requests handled? Are these requests submitted for clearance through liaisons first?

- What are the normal defaults for e-book ordering (e.g., single-user purchase option [SUPO] versus multiple-user purchase option [MUPO]; preferred vendor or platform; preferred format [is a PDF okay?])? How do you go about indicating changes to these defaults? Are these defaults based on policy or preference? Does cost matter?

TIMING IS EVERYTHING

Throughout this book, we talk about timing, be it turnaround times (TATs), cutoff dates, deadlines, or the like. Why such emphasis? It has been our experience over the past dozen years that liaisons who really work to understand and pay attention to the timing of various processes have a much easier time with this part of their responsibilities. When you are a liaison, you are balancing what might feel like a million different responsibilities; keeping up with them can be challenging, and missing a deadline or misunderstanding a TAT can decrease your effectiveness. Even though it's the last thing we mention in this chapter, it's one of the very first things you, as a liaison, should educate yourself about. And for those of you reading this book who aren't liaisons, be aware that keeping up with deadlines and other important dates can be very daunting for first-time or new-to-the-institution liaisons. Proactive communication from acquisitions can help liaisons be timely, especially when collection or budget deadlines loom at the same time liaisons are most busy with other responsibilities, such as teaching.

Timing and deadlines are definitely two topics you should address during face-to-face conversations with your acquisitions colleagues

> ## COLLEAGUES
>
> It's crucial to get deadline and timing information from acquisitions, but don't forget your liaison colleagues when seeking this information! They can clue you in to common liaison-specific issues that may occur around timing (e.g., final deadlines for ordering occur during the heaviest instruction time, professors and instructors always have last-minute requests) as well as provide you with advice or strategies for managing competing responsibilities.

(see the section "Organizational Structure" in this chapter). We advise you to ask about both soft and firm deadlines, how deadlines are determined, and how timing for other events arises. You may find that some events, such as the date the final budget is released to the library, are externally determined, and, therefore, the library has less flexibility in what happens and when. However, other times and dates are determined internally, and, therefore, you may find there's much more flexibility. It can take some time to figure out all the intricacies of important events and deadlines, so have some patience with yourself and your acquisitions colleagues if it takes you a year or two to get into the swing of things.

TIMING IS EVERYTHING
Questions You Should Be Asking

- When does ordering normally begin each year?
- When does ordering normally end for the year?
- Who sets these dates? How much flexibility is included in these dates? Are there grace periods? How are these dates determined?
- Can you explain how rush timing works?
- When should I expect dates for reversions or cuts to be announced? What happens if I've already spent all my funds?
- Are there routine cutoff dates?

- If special funds (end-of-year monies, for example) become available, what is the time line for submitting resource requests? What time(s) of year are these special funds most likely to become available?

- Are there specific times during the acquisitions cycle when justifications are considered for the purchase of resources that are not standard monographs (e.g., expensive one-time items, journals)? Are these set dates? Who sets them? How much notice will I receive?

- What is the normal TAT for e-books? Does this time vary by vendor?

- When can I modify or ask for modification to my approval plans? Do I have to have that done by a specific time, or can I do it anytime? How long will it take for modifications to be reflected in the approval plan?

4
Acquisitions Ordering

You may be thinking, "Hey, I'm a liaison and my job here is done. I've submitted my orders. Why would I need to know about what acquisitions does with them?" In our experience, liaisons are interested in resource arrival and availability, and if you understand how acquisitions ordering works, you will develop a sense of just how long it takes for specific resource types to become available, you won't annoy your acquisitions coworkers with the same "Now, when will this be here again?" questions over and over, and you will have the benefit of being able to translate complex, multistep acquisitions processes for patrons who want to know why you don't just "order it from Amazon already, for heaven's sake." And for our readers from the acquisitions world, remember that from a liaison's perspective, acquisitions ordering may seem like a foreign world with a different language and rules. Making sure that liaisons get the information they need without overloading them is key for fostering their understanding of the acquisitions process.

ORGANIZATIONAL STRUCTURE (AGAIN)

We outlined strategies for discerning the organizational and communication structure of acquisitions in chapter 3, "Submitting Orders," so we will refrain from repeating ourselves much here. It is crucial to remember, however, that the keys to learning are to talk to people and to ask questions instead of making assumptions; getting to know and understand who handles what in acquisitions is a multistep process that may take some time to comprehend. See the "Questions You Should Be Asking" section in chapter 3 regarding the organizational structure of acquisitions.

CHANGES AND REORGANIZATION

Remember that throughout the library, job functions sometimes shift from person to person or even unit to unit due to changes in personnel (shortages, unplanned outages) or reorganization by the administration. Sometimes these changes are just temporary, but it's not unusual for them to become permanent. Be prepared to stay abreast of these changes; just because acquisitions is organized a certain way this year doesn't mean that it won't change next year! Libraries aren't static entities, and effective liaisons remain alert to changes outside their own areas of interest and responsibility.

RECORD KEEPING AND COMMUNICATION

Acquisitions is also usually responsible for maintaining documentation related to ordering and for providing updates regarding ordering, including deadlines, spent fund amounts, and problems with orders or materials. Acquisitions should be able to provide liaisons with information about items that have been received but not yet processed and cataloged, orders that have been delayed because they are out of stock or backordered, and items that may not be coming anytime soon because they are not yet published. Liaisons depend on regular communications from acquisitions to keep them on-track during the ordering season, so it is important for liaisons to understand what information acquisitions tracks, what routine reports acquisitions runs and distributes, and how frequently reports are issued, among other things. As with all library departments, communications within and from acquisitions will likely be both formal and informal. We recommend starting by asking your acquisitions colleagues what reports are routinely generated for liaisons, how often (weekly, monthly, yearly), and by whom. It also helps to ask what kinds of data are included in the reports; ask for a sample report.

RECORD KEEPING AND COMMUNICATION

Questions You Should Be Asking

- What formal reports does acquisitions issue to liaisons?

- How often are these reports issued? Does this timing change during the year (e.g., more frequently as ordering deadlines approach)?

- What information is included? Do expenditure reports, for example, include only how much I've spent, or will I get a detailed list of everything I've ordered since the last report? If the report doesn't include this information, how can I get it?

- Are weekly and monthly reports summarized in a yearly report? If so, is the information in the yearly report any different or more or less detailed?

- If reports, particularly expenditure updates, aren't as frequent as I'd prefer, is there a way for me to investigate on my own?

- How up-to-date is the information that is sent out to liaisons? For example, for expenditure reports, what activity dates are reflected?

- Are reports for DDA items included within the routine reports, or are those reports separate?

- What kinds of reports are available for approval plans?

- Does acquisitions handle database or e-journal reports? If not, where do I go for that information?

ORDERING PROCESSES

Ordering materials for an institution is not as simple as it would be for a private individual. That distinction may be *the* fundamental misunderstanding that patrons have about the acquisitions process in an academic library. Patrons do not know and may not care that we have agreements with vendors which allow us to obtain materials for a lower cost than the list price, that licensing negotiations may have to occur before access is made available, or that funds are not available year-round. Patrons also don't see the additional layers of confusing and obstructive institutional bureaucracy that can complicate the ordering process. Patrons are very used to getting it now, but that is just not how the acquisitions process works for institutions like academic libraries. And though we may sympathize with our patrons, new liaisons need to free themselves of that why-can't-we-just-order-from-Amazon mind-set as quickly as possible.

Liaisons should consider that in most cases, acquisitions has likely streamlined the processes as much as possible within the confines of institutional requirements. For those who work for a public institution, requirements are often set forth not only by the institution but also by government. These requirements may lengthen or delay ordering or require record keeping that takes time to complete. There's also a good likelihood that acquisitions does order from Amazon or similar vendors under certain circumstances, but those are often quite specific and constrained. We're not saying that acquisitions processes cannot be clunky or outdated or frustrating (because

---

THE AMAZON MIND-SET

We say liaisons should not operate from the "Amazon" mind-set, but we don't recommend that liaisons and acquisitions colleagues just give up and blindly adhere to the status quo. Advocating for faster and less complex acquisition processes can result in real change for the better. The mantra here is this: operate from the pragmatic, advocate for the ideal.

they can be all those things). Rather, we're saying that you have to work within the framework and structure in place—like it or not. As with all the other processes we discuss, understanding how it works can be the key to making it work really well for you. If you understand the mechanics, you can use them to your advantage. Machiavellian? Maybe, but we still recommend it.

As you learn about the following specific acquisitions processes, keep in mind that processes can and do vary widely from library to library and that even within a library, processes are changeable as workflows are reconsidered or additional requirements are implemented (e.g., additional record keeping or additional levels of approval for e-resources). Of the many processes involved in acquisitions ordering, we've identified three with which liaisons should become especially familiar: pre-order searching, vendor selection, and licensing.

Pre-order searching is the term we use to describe acquisitions processes that ensure there is no ordering of duplicate items, among other things. Pre-order searching is generally done by an individual in acquisitions who checks orders after liaisons submit them by searching the catalog or other resources (database lists, etc.). Acquisitions staff are looking for duplications that would result in multiple copies within and across formats. Staff may also be checking whether older editions or newer editions are already available in the library's collections. If your institution has multiple libraries or is a member of a consortium, acquisitions staff may be trying to determine how many copies may already be in the system. This may also be the point

---

YOU CAN'T ALWAYS GET WHAT YOU WANT

During the ordering process, the acquisitions department occasionally discovers that particular resources cannot be supported by the library. There may be policies against purchasing resources that include expendables (i.e., single-use items) or electronic resources that may be downloaded only once. Be aware that some vendors or publishers aren't academic library friendly and that your library may not support obtaining those resources.

at which acquisitions staff flag items that appear to conflict with the collection development policy.

A note about duplication and pre-order searching: the library's efforts to avoid duplication are often complicated by the fact that many resources now come as part of a package and are not chosen individually. For example, some duplication occurs when the library obtains e-book sets or streaming video packages. It's not uncommon to find that these packages contain several items the library already owns. Consortial purchasing can also result in unintentional duplication because such purchases usually don't consider the holdings of individual libraries. The takeaway for liaisons is that acquisitions invests time in pre-order searching to limit the duplication of intellectual content—and to avoid paying for it twice—but some duplicate content will inevitably be purchased despite the acquisition department's best efforts.

Vendor selection can be a difficult process for liaisons to appreciate fully. The combination of factors that determine which vendor will be used and when can be bewildering. For example, acquisitions units may have a contract with a specific vendor (sometimes called a *jobber*) for print monographs and audiovisual materials while having contracts with several different vendors for e-books. There may be a hierarchical list for preferred database providers, too, and special vendors for out-of-print items or foreign-language tomes. The combinations are perhaps not endless, but plentiful. Liaisons don't necessarily need to understand the minutiae of providers, but it is useful to know that some providers are quicker than others when it comes to TATs, that complicated or problem orders may go through more than one vendor (thus lengthening the time to acquire), and that liaisons may or may not have much say in vendor selection. This last point may not be useful for monographs but may be important when it comes to database, e-book, or e-journal providers.

Licensing is a process particular to specific types of materials, mainly e-resources. Like vendor selection, licensing can be complex. The level of complexity often depends on the type of e-resource you are obtaining and from whom. For e-books, once your main vendors and their associated licensing agreements (who can use the resource and when, copyright restrictions, etc.) are in place, ordering individual items may be straightforward and painless for both liaisons and acquisitions. New databases tend to be more complicated because even if they come from the same vendor, there may be different permissions or restrictions on different resources that have to be hammered out between the library and the vendor. Liaisons usually don't need to be involved in the intricacies of license negotiation, but they should be aware that there can be bureaucratic or administrative holdups because of licensing agreements. Liaisons should also be cognizant of the kinds of issues that may fall in the "I need to know this" category, such as off-campus user restriction, log-in restrictions, or patron limitations. And acquisitions colleagues should be talking to liaisons to make sure they are informed about licensing issues that may affect patron access or usability of the resource.

ORDERING PROCESSES
Questions You Should Be Asking

- How long does pre-order searching take? Am I responsible for any of that?
- If pre-order searching does find a duplicate item in either the same format or across formats, how am I notified of that?
- If acquisitions staff find a newer edition during pre-order searching, do they just buy it or do they contact me for a decision? If they just buy it, will they notify me?
- How does ordering vary by format type?
- Is batch ordering (i.e., ordering a bunch of the same types of items at the same time) done?
- If acquisitions does place batch orders, what's the threshold for submitting orders? Does acquisitions require a certain amount of the same kind of material to be in the queue before submitting to the vendor?
- Does acquisitions prioritize how orders are placed? If so, what are the prioritization criteria?

- How are orders submitted? Is all ordering electronic?

- What vendors do we usually use? Do they offer us a discount? What is the average TAT for materials purchased from these vendors once orders are submitted?

- How long does it generally take to negotiate a license with a new vendor? What about licenses with established vendors from whom we already have several products?

- Do product licenses vary even though they may come from the same vendor? How will I be notified about licensing agreement changes that affect patron access?

- Are there categories of resources that cannot be supported by the library? How does acquisitions notify liaisons when such resources are discovered?

- What happens if the liaison orders a format that the library has not acquired before? Are there processes in place for reviewing the library's ability to support new formats?

TIMING IS EVERYTHING (AGAIN)

Though liaisons may be most interested in timing related to submitting orders, the timing and rhythms of acquisitions processes also can play an important role in liaison planning. As in chapter 3, "Submitting Orders," we suggest that you ask about key acquisitions deadlines during face-to-face conversations with your acquisitions colleagues. Even a rudimentary understanding of these deadlines can put liaison-centric deadlines into perspective and facilitate better planning. Be sure to ask about both big-picture deadlines and everyday deadlines. It can be tempting to focus solely on cutoff dates, rollovers, and the like, but the everyday rhythms are also critical in determining what gets done when.

Liaisons should also realize that some orders take longer than others for vendors and publishers to fill. For example, orders for out-of-print books often take longer to fill than do orders for recently published books, and foreign-language resources published overseas are less likely to be procured as quickly as domestically published, English-language resources.

TIMING IS EVERYTHING (AGAIN)

Questions You Should Be Asking

- How often are orders submitted to vendors (e.g., daily, weekly)?
- Does submission of orders vary by time of year? If so, what are the slow times and what are the busy times?
- After I submit an order, what is the average TAT to submitting it to a vendor?
- What types of resources usually arrive promptly? What types usually take longer than average?
- If approval of continuing resources is done by committee, how often does the committee meet to approve resources?
- If approval of continuing resources is the responsibility of one person, are decisions made routinely or as submission of requests occurs?
- What are dates for rollovers (i.e., items ordered this year that haven't arrived and expenditure for which will come out of next year's budget)?
- How long do unfilled orders remain in the system before the liaison is asked to determine if they should be abandoned?
- How often are rush orders processed?

5
Receiving and Processing

Receiving and processing are the two procedures that happen after materials have arrived but before they've been cataloged. Many of these procedures are extremely routine, such as property stamping or security strip addition, yet understanding them is still helpful to liaisons. Familiarity with these activities allows you to easily locate a resource shortly after it is received, expertly request expedited processing (and understand just what that entails), or request a collection change before the item hits the shelves—for example, from reference to your main stacks. If the processes associated with receiving and processing were not included in any of the training you received as a liaison, be sure to ask for at least an overview of how items move through these routine tasks. You can always ask for a more detailed description or demonstration later. And remember, every library will have its own unique wrinkles that determine when and how books are routed through the various points of the receiving process, and liaisons need to understand the method that is specific to their library. We know that learning all this can take some time if you're busy with other liaison duties, but we encourage you to put it on your to-do list.

RECEIVING AND PROCESSING PHYSICAL RESOURCES

Resources that have a concrete physical presence in the library may undergo a lot of handling before they actually make it to cataloging, and, from there, to the shelves. These processes often vary by format type, and format type may also dictate who in the library handles the receiving and processing for certain items. For what may seem, at first glance, like a simple series of steps (unpack, bug, stamp, repeat), the procedures related to receiving and processing physical materials can sometimes be quite intricate.

Books, Media, and Other Non-Serial Items

Physical items, such as print books or media resources, typically arrive in boxes, complete with an invoice. Receiving's first step is to unpack the boxes and examine items for completeness and damage while ensuring that every item listed on the invoice has actually been received. Only a small percentage of items are ever missing or damaged, but it happens frequently enough to require the careful examination of each shipment. Missing or damaged items do not move on to the next step in the receiving process and are not available to patrons while the library resolves problems. For items that pass inspection, the next step in the receiving process is invoicing. At invoicing, payments for purchases are sent to vendors or publishers, and the library's acquisitions system is updated to reflect payment. The item's status changes from "encumbered" to "paid," and, in some systems, the status of items in the library catalog changes from "on order" to "received" or "being processed." The liaison takeaway here is this: at some point in the receiving process, the catalog will be

THE EAGER PATRON

Until a physical item is cataloged and shelved, it is unavailable to patrons, even though, to them, it may not appear this way. Some always-eager patrons have been known to bombard liaisons with questions regarding received but uncataloged items: "Where is it?" "Can I have it?" "Does 'in process' mean it will be shortly on the shelf?" "How long will it be in processing?" These questions are *exactly* why we recommend that liaisons familiarize themselves with the process: you can answer all these questions swiftly with no need to check in with acquisitions each time a question arises.

updated to indicate a change in status—signaling to any interested parties that the item is now physically present within the library.

After items are unpacked and invoiced, most are tagged with a security device, stamped with library property stamps, and have library bar codes added (though bar codes are sometimes added later by catalogers). For items that come from vendors with shelf-ready cataloging, this processing is already completed, so the library has little actual processing to do. Some materials require additional or special processing, perhaps for preservation, security, or ease of access purposes. Nonbook materials—such as DVDs, CDs, kits, maps—are among the types of items that require additional processing, often including repackaging. This extra processing, which can require careful thought and creativity when dealing with items with multiple small pieces, for example, can take extra time. These tricky materials may be processed in the library unit responsible for keeping and servicing them, so be aware that processing doesn't always happen solely in technical services.

Materials sent through approval plans also undergo procedures related to receiving and processing. Approval plan items arrive in specially marked boxes and have their own invoice. Items are placed on shelves for review by the appropriate person (a liaison, it is hoped), where they are either accepted or rejected for addition to the library collection. Items that are accepted then undergo routine procedures associated with physical materials while the rejected items are re-packed for return to the vendor.

Serials

Receiving and processing for newspapers, magazines, journals, loose-leaf reports, and the like, are performed separately from the same processes for non-serial items and usually by a different group of people. The processes for newly acquired print serials (which need copy cataloging, at a minimum) also differ slightly from those for serials to which the library already subscribes (which need no cataloging). The print serials processing workflow reflects that of the non-serials in most ways: inspect to ensure item is correct, undamaged, and complete; affix property stamps, security devices, bar codes, labels, and so forth; shelve in appropriate location. The main difference—at least for liaisons—is that new issues for already established serials, rather than having new catalog records created for each issue, must be checked in to the library's serials management system during processing before an available status is reflected.

Collection Designation

One final processing aspect for liaisons to consider is that of collection designation—that is, in what collection (reference, main stacks, leisure reading) does this item belong? For some items, such as serials or maps, format will determine where the item goes. For others, the specific fund used for the order determines where an item will be located in the library. And for yet other materials, collection designation is performed during processing. Because collection location can be a surprisingly heated subject and because liaisons usually have opinions as to where certain kinds of things should go, we recommend that you go the extra step in figuring out all the *whos, hows,* and *whys.*

RECEIVING AND PROCESSING PHYSICAL RESOURCES

Questions You Should Be Asking

- Who is responsible for unpacking physical items? Are all items unpacked in the same place by the same people, or does this activity vary by item type?

- Are items unpacked as soon as they are received? Is there ever a delay? If items aren't unpacked immediately, for what reason(s)? During the busy time for receiving, how long might it take for items to be unpacked?

- Does invoicing happen as soon as a box is unpacked? Who is responsible for invoicing?

- Do receiving and invoicing happen in the same area of the library? If not, are the items physically moved when they go from unpacking to invoicing?

- How can I locate an item that is still being received or processed? Do I need to ask for permission or notify someone if I want to take it off the shelf to look at it?

- If your library catalog provides information on the status of materials, when does the item change from "ordered" (or similar wording) to "received"?

- Who is responsible for bugging, stamping, adding spine labels, and affixing bar codes to materials? Where are these activities carried out? Can liaisons view or review books during this process?

- What percentage of items received are shelf-ready? Are these items kept in a separate area during processing? At what point are they commingled with non–shelf-ready materials?

- What types of special processing happen in the library and to what kinds of materials? For example, where is media material processed, and what kinds of special handling are needed for these items (new containers, special security)? How are items with multiple pieces, such as kits and games, handled? Does each item get its own bar code and security device? How does this requirement affect processing time?

- What kinds of items are bound upon receipt? How long, from receipt to shipping to the bindery to return, does the binding process take? Are items sent one by one to the bindery, or is a minimum number required before they can be shipped? What will the catalog status reflect for these types of items? What if an item is awaiting shipment to the bindery but a patron needs it? How is that situation handled?

- Where are approval plan items received and processed? Are our approval items shelf-ready or not? In either case, at what point are they commingled with non–approval plan items?

- Are rejected approval plan items returned right away, or are they kept until there are several to send back in a shipment?

- Where are serials items received and processed?

- How long does it take to get a new journal title to the shelf?

- How long does it take to get a new issue of an existing journal to the shelf, once received in the library? How soon is the catalog record updated to reflect the newest holding?

- Is there a map or a chart that shows where materials are physically located at any particular point in the receiving and processing workflow? If not and I want or need to look at an item, how do I know where to look? Who should I ask?

- When is the majority of collection designation done at this library? Who is responsible for it? Do liaisons have any say in where things go?

- What criteria govern collection designation? Are these criteria ever updated or revised? What do I do if I disagree with the collection designation for a particular item? Is there a way to override automatic collection designation?

RECEIVING AND PROCESSING ELECTRONIC MATERIALS

Procedures for handling electronic materials differ from those for physical resources, and, depending on your library and its philosophy regarding e-resources (through how many avenues are they made accessible, for example), these processes run the gamut from simple to complicated and time-consuming. What happens and when it happens also depend on the type of e-resource—e-book, database, e-journal, streaming video—in question.

E-books

E-book receiving and processing may seem messy and arbitrary to liaisons because there are so many workflow combinations possible. These workflows fluctuate based on different e-book aspects, including whether items are ordered individually or in batches; whether the item in question is firm order (meaning, "Yes, order this regardless of use") or on-demand (meaning, "This purchase will be triggered by use"); or whether the item is part of a packaged set—say, by subject or discipline. Workflows also depend on where and how a library decides to make e-books available to patrons. For example, does your library include e-books in your catalog and, if you have one, a discovery layer? On e-readers? What about A–Z lists of resources?

The truth is that there is no pat answer to the question, "How long does it take for an e-book I order to become available to patrons?" Sit down with your technical services colleagues and discuss the most common scenarios for e-books in your institution and then go from there. Build a general awareness of where the lags occur in the e-books workflow, but be prepared to receive (and give, if you are asked) a response of "It depends" when discussing e-books.

Databases and E-journals

The receiving and processing workflows related to new databases, e-journals, and even large e-book packages differ from those for individual e-books. Once the resource is ordered, appropriate licensing agreements are signed, and the resource is activated by the vendor, any paraphernalia used to manage and provide access to these electronic resources must be configured. The list is long and may include making additions or changes, or both, to proxy servers, link resolvers, discovery services, catalogs, database lists, and so on. These responsibilities may be shared or may be handled by just one person. Be sure to ask because you'll then know who to talk to should you have a question about set up. In addition, knowing the workflow can help you better understand how or why it may take some time before a "technically available" resource is "officially available" to patrons.

For existing e-resource content available through vendors, particularly content available through databases, be aware that the mix of resources may be constantly changing depending on the vendor's arrangements with individual content providers. New titles or new dates of coverage may be added constantly, or an item that you know you've seen before may mysteriously disappear. We suggest asking your technical services colleagues how often the catalog, discovery service, or other library resource is updated to reflect these changes.

RECEIVING AND PROCESSING ELECTRONIC MATERIALS
Questions You Should Be Asking

- Are individual non-DDA e-book orders processed separately or as a batch? If they are a batch, is a minimum number needed before the batch is handled?

- Are individual DDA e-book orders processed separately or as a batch? If they are a batch, is a minimum number needed before the batch is handled?

- Once the vendor-supplied cataloging records are received by the library, how soon do individual e-book titles become available to patrons? What is the patron-availability TAT for ordered e-books that *do not* have vendor-supplied cataloging records?

- What would make processing times longer for individual e-books?
- For items that go on particular devices, such as e-readers, when does the catalog record appear (before, after, or simultaneously with access to the item on the device)?
- Are individual titles that go on devices added to the device as they are received, or are these items batch added? If they are added when there are enough to form a batch, how many titles make up a batch?
- For electronic resources such as databases, e-journal packages, or e-book packages, what are the main steps of the processing workflow that are time-consuming (e.g., entering an item into an A–Z or subject list, proxying links, and so on)?
- Are all the steps for processing e-resources performed by the same person or unit? What is the normal TAT from activation to availability?
- When new e-resources that aggregate content—databases, for example—appear in patron lists (A–Z or subject database lists, e-journal lists), several questions will be pertinent:
    - ◊ Who is responsible for adding these resources to lists?
    - ◊ How do these lists get created?
    - ◊ Is populating these lists with titles mostly automated?
    - ◊ For subject lists, does the library control to which subject(s) a resource is assigned? Does subject assignment depend on the type of resource (database, e-journal, e-book, etc.)?
    - ◊ If the process is not automated for some (or all) subject lists, who determines the criteria for inclusion for specific subjects? Do liaisons have any say in nonautomated processes?
- As part of the processing, are records for e-resources added to the library catalog? If so, when does this occur and who is responsible for adding them? Will an item be available in patron lists before, after, or simultaneously with the cataloging of the item?

- How does the library handle changes in existing e-resources when the content changes? What library resource lists (catalog, discovery service, A–Z list) have to be updated when content changes? Are any of those processes automatic? How often are library resource lists updated with these kinds of changes? Is updating routine or irregular?

6
Cataloging

ataloging is fundamentally important to libraries of all types. Organization and description of resources enables everyone, both patrons and librarians, to find information. Understanding *how* cataloging works helps liaisons use the catalog and other tools more effectively while also enabling liaisons to communicate and work with catalogers to increase the effectiveness of information retrieval tools. When it comes to ensuring that information is discoverable, liaisons and catalogers are on the same team. Our goal is to help liaisons develop an understanding of processes and use this understanding to facilitate more efficient and speedy work; the key to this goal within cataloging is to understand the local cataloging workflow and the responsibilities, authority, and expertise of individual catalogers. For example, catalogers may specialize by format, by language, and, in very large libraries, by subject. Because of this specialization, one individual might not be able to rush catalog a particular

> ### CALLING CATALOGERS!
>
> Although this book's audience is mostly liaisons, we encourage catalogers to learn about the reference aspect of liaison work and to take advantage of the liaison's knowledge of patron needs and foibles when searching for information. Spending some time at the reference desk—either shadowing or fielding questions—can be a great way to learn how patrons understand and attempt to find information and how the information contained in catalog records can affect success.

item for you or make a desired enhancement. We highly recommend understanding who is responsible for what type of cataloging; it is much easier to get questions answered or to request enhancements when you can talk directly to the responsible individual.

COPY AND ORIGINAL CATALOGING

Modern cataloging units are process-oriented operations tasked with performing both copy and original cataloging. *Copy cataloging,* or using records already created by other cataloging agencies or vendors, allows cataloging departments to add large numbers of catalog records for many different material types. These pre-created catalog records, such as for electronic resources or for shelf-ready items, are often added to the catalog in large batch loads or through other automated processes. This procedure means many, many catalog records are added to the catalog without being examined by an actual human being in the library. Records that are inspected may be checked only to ensure that they match the resources being cataloged; these records are likely not checked closely for quality, completeness, or appropriateness. The small percentage of records that are closely examined are often those that are substandard or incomplete. When good copy cataloging records are available, processing moves quickly; some processing may even take place in a non-cataloging unit, such as acquisitions. University press books, best-selling trade books, and

AUTHORITY CONTROL, AACR2, RDA, MARC

Many liaisons may worry that we'll recommend understanding all the intricacies of how a catalog record is created–a truly daunting task! Although we won't discourage anyone from brushing up on cataloging knowledge, here are the technical terms with which liaisons should be familiar:

Authority control: Consistent use of one form of a name, subject, or title heading and referring alternate forms to that established form. Good authority control makes everything in the catalog easier to find.

AACR2: Cataloging rules pre-2013.

RDA: Cataloging rules post-2013.

MARC: A set of standards that allows computers to read and share bibliographic data. When catalogers talk about 100s, 245s, and 650s, they are referring to MARC fields where cataloging data exist.

other popular resources are examples of items likely to have good copy cataloging and thus a quick arrival-to-shelf time.

Original cataloging is creating a catalog record completely from scratch and is done by fully trained catalogers. This type of cataloging is generally performed for items that lack any existing catalog record; materials that most often fall in this category include items that are in unusual formats or a foreign language—or resources that may have been produced locally. Original cataloging is a longer and more complex process than copy cataloging; it involves determining what information is needed and which fields to use, and it may involve consultation of many different sources to create a complete, robust, and accurate record. In light of the potential amount of work original cataloging can require, liaisons should adjust TAT expectations accordingly.

Both original and copy cataloging have their own workflows that will vary due to different factors, including time of year, position vacancies, training, or changes to cataloging standards. Backlogs of both high- and low-priority materials may exist, so you will want to talk to your colleagues about how those are classified and handled. We also recommend talking to your cataloging unit about how to handle rush cataloging. Some items are rushed through the entire process, from ordering to patron checkout, but some items become a priority only after arriving at the library. Be sure to find out how (and from whom) to request rush cataloging. Because there is often a backlog of materials to be cataloged, be sensitive to how frequently you ask for this service from catalogers; overuse of requesting rush processes dilutes the effectiveness of asking for true rush requests.

COPY AND ORIGINAL CATALOGING
Questions You Should Be Asking

- How are cataloging responsibilities divided (e.g., by format, language, subject)? Who is responsible for each type?
- Who is responsible for original cataloging? Who is responsible for copy cataloging? How does this division work if cataloging responsibilities are further divided by type (format, subject, etc.)?
- What is the average TAT based on material type?
- What is the average TAT for items that have good copy cataloging records?
- What is the average TAT for items that have incomplete or substandard cataloging records that have to be fixed?
- What is the average TAT for items that need original cataloging?
- What times of the year does copy cataloging move more slowly? What does the TAT usually average at that point? Where are items not yet cataloged physically located?
- What are the procedures for requesting a rush cataloging job? In what circumstances would I have to tell a patron we cannot rush catalog an item?
- How is cataloging for electronic resources handled? Are all electronic resources, including databases, added to the catalog? Does

the process differ by e-resource type (e.g., DDA items, large record sets)? How long does it usually take?

- How are DDA items identified in the catalog? Can I tell by looking at a record if an item is DDA?

- How is cataloging handled for items received through an approval plan? Is the TAT different than it is for other items?

- Are there backlogs of uncataloged resources in addition to the ones awaiting copy cataloging? Is there a way to identify and locate resources that are in the backlog?

- If I notice an error in the catalog record, who do I notify? How long does it take to change the record? Are there any circumstances in which an incorrect record can't be changed? If so, what are they?

- Some catalogs allow libraries to incorporate remote external content, such as contents notes or book cover images, in the catalog display, even though this content is not part of the actual catalog record. How can I tell when such content has been added? What kind of control do we have over that information? What should I do if I notice that the added content is incorrect?

- Some e-resource information—licensing restrictions on simultaneous users, for example—is not added to nor contained within an item's catalog record. Where is that information recorded, and who maintains it? How is this information made available to liaisons when access questions arise?

ENHANCING CATALOGING RECORDS

Cataloging, both original and copy, is governed by national and international standards that set forth how catalog records are constructed. These rules describe what information is required for each record and how that information is structured and arranged. These standards allow cataloging records to be shared from library to library and integrated into local library catalogs, regardless of the

CATALOGING STANDARDS

The application of national standards to cataloging may give an impression that all catalog records are of uniform consistency and quality. This is simply not the case. Standards have changed significantly over time and continue to evolve; just look at cataloging records that have been added to your local catalog over time. Many conform to historical standards and practices but not necessarily to the current standards. As a result, be aware that you may encounter inconsistent or strange records in the catalog.

origination of the catalog record. Catalogers are very sensitive to following these standards and guidelines so that work can be shared among libraries. The rules that may seem nitpicky, confusing, or even unnecessary to liaisons often make sense in the context of greater sharing among libraries. The good news is that although there are many rules and standards to which catalogers must adhere, they can still do a lot to customize records and make the catalog more useful for both liaisons and library users.

Individual Record Editing

The easiest changes tend to be single, one-time revisions that improve an individual catalog record. Catalogers, with a minimal amount of effort, can enhance many parts of a record. We could talk about these enhancements at length, but the two of most interest to liaisons are changing or adding to note fields and creating additional access points through headings.

Note fields provide additional information about a resource; depending on the item, notes can range from grade-level appropriateness to a list of a film's cast to awards received to a summary of the subject matter. Notes are not governed by controlled vocabulary and so provide more flexibility when describing a resource. A note type of particular interest to liaisons is the *contents note* wherein every chapter in a book, every volume in a multivolume set, every song on a compact disc, and so forth, is listed. Contents notes are extremely useful because they not only provide additional information to anyone using the catalog but also improve access to the material by providing content discoverable by keyword search.

Headings, such as title, author, and subject, are ways to facilitate finding an item in the catalog. In the past, cataloging standards dictated a limit to the number of "official" headings in catalog records (you may see this rule reflected in older catalog records). That practice has changed with new standards; however, the number and type of headings initially added are still often a matter of the cataloger's judgment. If you determine that a record lacks sufficient description, especially information that is of interest or importance to your community of patrons, ask a cataloger to enhance individual records by creating additional headings that will serve as extra access points.

A final note on notes and headings: common sense dictates strategic employment of additional notes and fields. Enhanced description is a wonderful thing, but include too many extras and you end up with a record that isn't very useful because it's cluttered with irrelevant information. Collaborate with your cataloging colleagues to employ these two powerful enhancements wisely.

Batch Editing

Catalogers also engage in projects where they fix or enhance large numbers of existing cataloging records. When the change is the same for each record, automated processing is possible; if the change is straightforward, a multi-record (batch) edit may be accomplished in just one afternoon. Unfortunately for both liaisons and catalogers, many multi-record projects aren't quite that easy and instead require catalogers to review and make judgments about one record at a time. In these cases, project difficulty depends on both the batch size and the complexity of the requested changes or enhancements. Often these complicated projects are not a priority and may languish during busy times. If you have identified a project that requires editing a large number of items, it's best to determine the exact set that needs changing and the specific change(s) desired before approaching cataloging. Liaisons should also be prepared to work with catalogers during the project to help make judgment calls on vocabulary, granularity, and prioritization. If a project is beyond the capabilities of the local cataloging unit, usually as a result of a lack of resources or expertise, outsourcing may be considered.

Workflow Edits

Some records enhancements have long-term, ripple effects on cataloging workflow. Because these changes usually require altering standard operating procedures, often for just a subset of materials, requests that require them often undergo extra scrutiny and aren't implemented without considerable discussion. And what may seem like a simple request for just a few items may result in disruptions to established processes, require changes in documentation, necessitate additional training for catalogers, and slow the automated processing of copy-cataloging materials. Also, because a new procedure for a subset of materials may directly contradict established procedures for all other materials, catalogers have to increase vigilance when cataloging to ensure that each type of material is handled correctly.

Although one change to the basic workflow may not seem like a big deal to a liaison, many instances of special treatment for different kinds of material have the cumulative effect of slowing the entire cataloging process. This doesn't mean that cataloging processes should never be changed; enhancements that address serious patron access issues but that also have an impact on established workflow should be implemented when necessary. We urge thoughtfulness and restraint when making these requests though, because cataloging workflows cannot accommodate every special treatment request.

ENHANCING CATALOGING RECORDS
Questions You Should Be Asking

- What kinds of changes to individual records will catalogers make upon request? What is the process for requesting such changes?

- Who in the cataloging department is responsible for making changes to records?

- What controlled vocabularies are used in the catalog as access points? Is there a thesaurus or list for these vocabularies that liaisons can consult before requesting another access point?

- What is the process for requesting a project that will involve changes to many records?

- How large a project can the cataloging unit realistically be expected to complete?

- Are there periods during the year that the cataloging unit customarily has time to complete large projects?

- When a patron performs a keyword search in the catalog, what are the default fields (title, author, contents notes, etc.) searched?

- When additional access points are needed, what is the process for adding local authors or local geographic subject headings?

- When the same change is required for many records, does the liaison or the cataloger identify the set of records to be processed? Do they work together to create a set of records for batch editing? If so, what is this process?

- If we share a catalog with other institutions, how does batch editing affect them? Do we have to get permission to do this?

ENHANCING THE CATALOG ITSELF

Liaisons and catalogers can affect the patron experience positively when working together to make edits, changes, and enhancements to resource records. The liaison–cataloger collaboration can continue on a big-picture level: enhancement of the catalog itself. Many libraries continuously strive to optimize the overall experience for their patrons, be that by integrating other resources, improving the catalog record display, or changing search limits, modifiers, or scopes. Liaisons and catalogers can contribute to this effort by building on what the liaison has experienced through interactions with patrons and through the liaison's own searches as well as the cataloger's fundamental knowledge of information organization and classification—both its possibilities and its limitations.

We realize that new liaisons working with new systems may not yet know what enhancements would be desirable or possible; even seasoned liaisons with a good knowledge of their catalog's strengths and flaws may not be exactly sure of what can be changed. Don't let this lack of information deter you, though, even if it seems daunting at first. Start by keeping a list of big-picture things that you'd like to see changed or that you don't understand, talk to your liaison and cataloging colleagues to get an idea of the catalog's background and known limitations, and *participate* in catalog discussions, task forces, and committees. Getting yourself involved as a liaison in catalog discussions is a great way to get a better understanding of how your catalog system works and to advocate for improved patron (and librarian) experience within that system.

ENHANCING THE CATALOG ITSELF
Questions You Should Be Asking

- Who provides our catalog? If we buy our system, what vendor provides the software?
- Is it possible for the library to configure or make changes to the catalog's web interface?

- Are there any changes to the catalog interface we are unable to make? If yes, why?

- How much control does the library have over what information within the technical (MARC) record is displayed as part of the online catalog record? Can the order in which the fields are displayed be changed? Can some fields be suppressed? What exactly can be changed and what can't?

- Is it possible to change the way the catalog's search function works? Is it possible to change what MARC fields are searched by keyword or other types of searches? For example, if the names of performers that appear in notes in records for compact discs are not retrieved by a keyword search, is it possible to change the configuration of the system so they will be?

- What other searches, beyond basic author, title, and keyword searches, can be created?

- If we can create additional indexes, are we allowed to specify what fields within the record are included in these indexes?

- When changes are both permitted and technically possible, ask the following questions:

  ◊ What is the process for requesting changes, and is that process documented for liaisons?

  ◊ Who is in charge of receiving, reviewing, and implementing changes or configurations? Is an individual or a group in charge?

  ◊ How frequently are change requests reviewed? How long does it take to implement a change?

  ◊ Are past decisions ever reviewed? If so, are reviews periodic, or does someone have to request a review?

  ◊ Is technical documentation available that helps explain how changes are made? Are catalogers and other technical staff available to help me use such documentation?

7
Collection Maintenance

ollection maintenance is not just a fancy term for weeding, we promise! It includes weeding, of course, but also collection changes and format updates. This maintenance is a vital part of a liaison's responsibilities, though it often falls to the bottom of the priority list when other needs press. However, collection maintenance ensures that the collection accurately and appropriately reflects the needs of the user community. This fundamental concept is one that liaisons should prioritize even when other responsibilities loom.

The decision making and processes required to perform comprehensive collection maintenance are intricate, usually take a lot of time and brainpower, and require a collective effort between liaisons and technical services staff. Be prepared for the process to be slow on occasion as well as iterative. In this chapter, we're not going to focus on how-do-I-make-decisions or best practices for decision making.

TO OPINE FOR JUST ONE MOMENT

Collection maintenance is a job that is never truly completed because it is more than simply a series of tasks to be checked off a list. It's an important, if sometimes frustrating, aspect of liaisonship that we think deserves serious time and thoughtfulness from liaisons. To that end, we encourage you to (to borrow a motto) be prepared. Think about collection maintenance and what information you want or need to know, particularly for weeding, so that should projects be suddenly initiated with short deadlines and lofty goals, decision making is driven by more than a need to just get things done.

There are myriad resources for that in the literature, and opinions abound. Instead, we'll focus on the processes that often go along with collection maintenance as they relate to technical services. And because collection maintenance is a collective effort that involves technical services, understanding these processes makes accomplishing those types of tasks much easier.

WEEDING

Weeding is probably the best known and most discussed aspect of collection maintenance, and, as a liaison, you will almost certainly be expected to participate in, if not lead, weeding projects. Thoughtful weeding enables libraries to maintain their collections according to their library's values and mission by elimination of old, inaccurate, or irrelevant information, reduction of clutter, and identification of damaged or lost materials. Weeding projects are also initiated to address physical space issues common to most libraries.

Despite the benefits associated with the process, weeding is sometimes controversial within the library. Dissension can often be attributed to philosophical differences within the library or even between the library and those it serves. Although we won't wade into how to navigate those waters, we do think it's important to be aware that weeding can be a fraught process and that educating yourself about past projects—including missteps and triumphs—is crucial to future success. And though weeding can be a contentious issue, it's important to recognize it is a necessity for almost all libraries. Weeding—or deselecting, if you prefer—has many aspects. In this book, we'll focus on the planning, decision-making, and processing aspects that involve both the liaison and technical services.

Initiation and Planning

Weeding projects are initiated for many reasons. As a liaison, you may want to initiate a weeding project to update your collection areas, to help identify areas of weakness, or to adhere to accreditation standards. Others in the library may initiate weeding with an eye toward making space, removing duplicate resources, or streamlining and updating the collection as a whole. Regardless, there are planning steps that must happen before decision making begins. These steps include identifying goals, hard and soft targets, and an ideal time line. Part of this plan may also include identifying other decision makers to consult during weeding, such as other liaisons who are responsible for related areas or subject-specific teaching or research faculty. Ask your technical services colleagues for help in identifying these steps if there isn't an existing guide for initiating a project, and definitely talk to liaison colleagues about any unofficial steps you'll want to consider as you plan your weeding project.

Weeding requires collaboration across units; if you initiate a project, you must consult with colleagues, particularly those in technical services. Not only is this just good practice (and considerate), it ensures that all necessary partners are informed and that everyone has time to plan workloads and workflows as appropriate or to provide feedback so any issues can be addressed before a project begins. Again, there may be a guide for you already in place regarding who to notify and how, but if not, talk to both technical services and liaison colleagues so you can identify the *who* and the *how*.

Finally, don't forget that all projects require documentation—likely both formal and informal. You'll need to have a good grasp of the required paperwork before you begin or you could end up with a confusing mess, or you may find yourself trying to reconstruct information for a report well after your weeding is finished. Be absolutely sure you talk to your collection development librarian or similar authority about the documentation and record keeping that will be required during the planning, implementation, and completion stages. And as you begin your first project, ask other liaisons if they keep any records in addition to those required by technical services. You may get some really great ideas this way.

Decision Making

Decision making is the most arduous and perhaps most painful part of the weeding process, and that's probably why there is so much how-to literature out there that includes best practices as well as philosophical musings on weeding. We'll spare you our opinions on all that (we definitely have opinions, though) and instead focus on two of the more technical aspects of decision making: statistics and collaborators.

Most, if not all, weeding decision making is going to include gathering and using statistics based on certain metrics. Some of the metrics—total checkouts, total downloads, or publication date, for example—might be automatically included in reports whereas other metrics might be important to you but not necessarily to technical services staff or other colleagues. For example, when weeding physical items in the general stacks collection, technical services may routinely provide statistics on the number of checkouts and renewals or the age of the item. But other information, such as the date of the last checkout or the number of internal circulations, may not be provided unless specifically requested. Before starting any project, consult with technical services regarding the metrics that are automatically included and those that are considered optional but which can be requested. And remember that standard metrics vary by item type or format, so the information you receive for an e-journal may be different than the information you receive for that same title in print. Developing a go-to list of metrics for specific weeding types involves a bit of trial and error, but don't be afraid to seek out this additional information, especially during your first few attempts at weeding.

As previously mentioned, in addition to developing metrics profiles, you'll need to identify any individuals with whom you must consult about a specific weeding project. Your collections policy might stipulate that teaching faculty must review physical items or the list of e-resources selected for weeding. Or perhaps you are considering weeding in an interdisciplinary area that is of interest to multiple liaison colleagues. No matter who you consult, make sure you understand any official process for collecting and recording feedback as well as how that feedback may be weighed when compared with other factors. Whether or not you seek feedback for weeding decisions from others, be aware that programs accredited by official bodies may have certain collections requirements in order to meet the accreditor's standards—the American Chemical Society (ACS) accreditation for chemistry programs is a good example. Be sure you review accreditors' collections guidelines and expectations before moving forward with any collections decisions.

A last note about decision making: ask your collection development colleagues if your weeding decisions are reviewed; if so, by whom; and exactly how the review process works. It may be that only your first project or two will be reviewed by the collection

HANDS-ON DECISION MAKING

Decision making for physical items is likely to include, at times, a hands-on review of the materials. Sometimes this review may involve just you as the liaison while at other times it may involve you and teaching or research faculty. Be sure to ask your technical services colleagues how in-person review is handled (where are the items placed, how long do you have to review, etc.). We also recommend getting advice from liaison colleagues who have previously participated in physical reviews, especially reviews conducted with teaching or research faculty participation. These colleagues can provide invaluable advice particularly when it comes to setting reasonable expectations and avoiding common pitfalls.

development librarian, or you may find that projects are reviewed each time you finish. And the review could vary from spot-checking your decisions to conducting an in-depth examination. If your list is reviewed before any further steps are taken toward withdrawal, you will want to ask how differences of opinion are resolved as well as how you will be notified of any changes to your decisions or recommendations.

Withdrawal Processes

After all the decisions are made, it's time for the nitty-gritty part of the weeding process: withdrawal. Withdrawal is the act of removing the item from both physical and virtual locations. For withdrawal of physical items, we think that liaisons should concentrate on the *who, when,* and *where.* After withdrawal lists are created, you will want to know who is responsible for the process of removing these items from shelves, how long it takes from initiating the withdrawal to actual removal of the item from all spaces (physical and virtual), and where these items are stored as they await withdrawal processing. You may find on rare occasions that you need to track down an item that has been removed from the physical location but not yet completely withdrawn, or perhaps you see that search results in the catalog still reflect items you know were slated for withdrawal. Familiarity with the withdrawal processes of your technical services colleagues enables you to understand why these situations occur as well as how and when you can expect them to be resolved. A final note about withdrawal of physical items: we strongly recommend that liaisons ask about current withdrawal backlogs when a weeding project is initiated. Backlogs mean that the TAT for withdrawals could take much longer than you would normally expect; planning for longer TATs can help you pace your project accordingly or even delay it if the backlog is severe.

Withdrawal processes for e-resources differ somewhat because there is no physical item to remove from a shelf; only virtual locations exist for e-resources. For withdrawals of e-materials, you'll still want to know who is responsible for removing items from virtual spaces (this can be multiple people, depending on the space: catalog, A–Z list, discovery layer, etc.), and how long it will take from initiation to completion. You will want to ask, especially if multiple individuals are involved, what the liaison's role is in notifying everyone that an item is to be removed. It may be that once you turn in your withdrawal list for e-items to collection development, staff in that department will initiate all removal and you need to do nothing else. Or you may find yourself responsible for requesting removal from certain lists or guides.

For both electronic and physical resources, be sure you know who to approach if you see an item listed that you are positive has been withdrawn. This person also will be an important contact in case a mistake is made. For example, if the wrong item was removed—the eighth edition instead of the sixth—you will need to know who to ask to restore the correct item to the shelf, a particular list, or the catalog.

WEEDING

Questions You Should Be Asking

- Has the library instituted a regularly scheduled collection review process that includes weeding? If so, what are the parameters for this process?

- What collections are normally considered part of the liaison's responsibility to weed? Are liaisons only responsible for weeding the main stacks collection, or are they also responsible for other areas, such as the reference collection, individual e-journals, and so on? If liaisons do not have responsibility for other collections, who should be consulted when items in those collections need to be removed?

Initiation and Planning

- Who generally initiates weeding? Is it primarily liaison driven?

- Is there a formal procedure for setting the goals, process, and time line? Where can I find the documentation that outlines this procedure?

- Does the library outline standards that I must use for collection review? If so, what are they?

- How and to whom does a liaison give feedback regarding any changes to the weeding process or timing of weeding projects?

- For a project that is liaison initiated, who in technical services (or elsewhere) needs to be notified, and how much notice is required before beginning?

- If a project is initiated by someone else (i.e., not a liaison) in the library, how long does the planning phase last? On average, how much notification will I receive before needing to begin a project?

- What documentation is required of liaisons for weeding projects? Are there guidelines or specific forms for this documentation?

Metrics, Statistics, and Data

- At what point do liaisons receive data for items under review?

- Who provides these data?

- What default metrics are reported? How does this vary by format?

- Can liaisons generate this information themselves? If so, who provides the liaison training?

- If the data cannot be retrieved by a liaison, who can access them?

- What is the process for obtaining additional data if the first set retrieved is not adequate for decision making?

- In what format will the data be presented (.csv, .xlsx, etc.)?

- What is the level of granularity of the data? For example, would statistics for e-resources indicate the numbers of downloads by publication year or just overall downloads?

- Do I receive the raw data for the metrics requested? If not, what is done to the data before I receive them?

- What kinds of data are unavailable or not recorded by the library (e.g., access by patron type, checkouts by month or year, etc.)?

- Are statistics for duplicate formats (print, electronic) reported together or separately? If duplicate formats include an e-resource,

will there be an indication of whether the e-resource is acquired
through subscription or purchase?

- How are the data handled for multipart items (volumes, monographic series, etc.)? Are the data reported by item or in the
aggregate? How are the parts denoted in the data?

- How are the data reported for issues related to item history?
For example, how are title changes (preceding and succeeding
titles) or preceding and subsequent editions identified in weeding
reports or lists? If item history is not identifiable through standard
weeding data, what is the best way to obtain this information?

Faculty and Liaison Feedback

- Is the teaching and research faculty role in review or weeding processes specified in collection development policy?

- If not, what are some ways to solicit feedback from faculty members that have been successfully used in the past?

- If so, what is the process (procedures, time lines, and documentation)? What is the weight given to faculty feedback when compared to statistics and other opinions?

- If there is a formal process that requires faculty feedback, how do
I handle situations where I receive no feedback? What is the best
way to document these instances?

- How much wiggle room is there regarding faculty review deadlines? If faculty members continually miss deadlines, at what point
am I allowed to end their part of the process?

- How do I handle it if faculty feedback is "keep everything" or if
faculty members fundamentally disagree with the weeding processes? What kind of support does collection development provide when I encounter recalcitrant faculty?

- If a decision comes down to faculty versus liaison, who makes the
final decision? Who makes that call?

- How is weeding handled within interdisciplinary subjects? For
example, both the health sciences and the science liaisons have

an interest in anatomy; who is primarily responsible for weeding this section? How is this determined? What mechanisms are in place for sharing collection review responsibilities?

- What if someone is weeding in her own area and I disagree with a decision? Is there a process to appeal? What if I really think the person is making a mistake? Who makes the final determination?

Withdrawal Processes

- What documentation do I need to submit to begin the withdrawal process? Who do I notify that the documentation is ready and that withdrawal can begin?

- Who should I ask about withdrawal backlogs and their estimated time to resolution? Should I wait to submit withdrawal decisions until backlogs are cleared?

- Are items that will be physically reviewed pulled from the shelf by the liaison or by someone else? If the latter, by whom? Is there a procedure if I prefer to pull my own items?

- For physical items, is there a specific to-be-reviewed shelf for under-review items once they are pulled from the stacks? Are these items updated in the catalog with a new location or status, such as "in technical services" or "under review"?

- After items on the to-be-reviewed shelves have been reviewed, where do they go? Are there shelves for items that will be retained and for items that will be weeded? Where are these shelves located?

- After I have submitted a list of resources for withdrawal, how soon does a physical item come off the shelf?

- After I have submitted a list of resources for withdrawal, how long will it take to eliminate their virtual presence?

- For items that require both physical and virtual handling, is the virtual or physical presence the first to go?

- What happens to the physical items we remove from the collection?

- What should I do about items that I can't find in the collection and that are on my to-be-considered list (i.e., they are missing)? Should I report these as I normally would any lost item?

- What happens if I make a mistake and include something that shouldn't be withdrawn? Is there any mechanism for someone to check behind me?

LOCATION CHANGES

As we stated earlier, collection maintenance is not just about weeding your collections. It also encompasses moving resources from one collection to another, both physically and virtually. Examples of location changes include books that were once reference but now need to go into the general collection; unique or valuable items that should go into special collections, archives, or closed stacks; or updated e-resources that need to be added to or removed from subject lists online. Location changes can also be part of a larger project as new collections are created or as older collections are folded into other existing collections.

Our first suggestion is to inquire about any circumstances that trigger automatic location changes. For example, it's unlikely that an item will stay in a New Books or New Arrivals location indefinitely or that current periodicals don't get bound or microfilmed at a certain point. What guidelines govern how long an item stays in those collections before it makes its way to another location? If you know when and how things are automatically relocated, you may more easily track down something that doesn't have an absolutely up-to-date location in your catalog (hey, it happens!) or at least make a reasonable guess as to where it may be.

You'll also want to ask about liaison-initiated changes to either individual items or sets of items to find out if a process is in place for requesting location changes. It's useful to understand how many people you may have to consult for particular item types, how long it might take them, and what reasons exist for your request to be denied. As you work through both automatic and on-demand collection changes, remember that materials are relocated to keep collections up to date and to make sure that the collections themselves contain suitable materials.

LOCATION CHANGES

Questions You Should Be Asking

- What collections in the library have an automatic relocation policy? What triggers (date, use, trial status) govern that relocation?
- When items are moving from one physical location to another:
  ◊ How long does it take for the items to go from the old shelf to their new location?
  ◊ Who moves them?
  ◊ Is there any intermediary storage place if they don't move directly? Where is that?
  ◊ Under what circumstances are these items relabeled?
- How long does it take a catalog record (or similar) to be updated to reflect the new location?
- What are the steps for moving an e-resource item either onto or off a list or collection? How quickly can this relocation happen?
- If a liaison wants to initiate a location change, what are the steps for that? Does it depend on the collections affected? Do liaisons always need to consult with collection development if they want to move a single item? What about multiple items or large sets?
- Are there any reasons that items would not be moved to another location when requested by a liaison?
- Are there any reasons that items in collections that are normally automatically moved to another location (triggered by date, checkouts, etc.) wouldn't get moved? For example, is there ever a time an item would stay in New Books or in Current Periodicals past the time it would normally be moved to the stacks?

- What about items, such as journals or newspapers, that have to be bound or microfilmed before they change collections? For those that go to a bindery, is there a set schedule? How can I tell if something is at the bindery rather than here and waiting to be shipped to the bindery? What is the TAT for standard bindery items?

- For items, such as local newspapers, that are replaced by microfilm copies, how long does it take for a microfilm copy to replace the print? How quickly is the record updated to show a change in location? How quickly is the item removed from the shelf once the microfilm is received?

FORMAT UPDATES

A key part of collection maintenance is dealing with format changes caused by the evolution of technology. Think of the evolution of motion picture film to VHS tapes (or Betamax) to DVDs and the differences in the equipment required for each format type. Progress in this area is often a double edged sword for libraries and their patrons. New technologies make it easier to access and use resources; at the same time, older yet still valuable resources may not be available through the newer technology. Additionally, items available only in these vanishing formats often require special equipment to be usable. Some libraries are committed to maintaining equipment to handle aged formats, such as motion picture film, 8-track tapes, or opaque microcards, but many cannot and are faced with the need to update a format. Changing (or updating) formats is also not free; to re-create an entire collection, say, of LP records does not come cheaply or without effort.

We recommend that you start by asking about unusual or vintage formats in the library and what the policy is for maintaining or replacing those. You may find that there are very few of these types of items in your subject areas, but you'll still want to know for any patrons who may inquire. If you are responsible for collections that have these aging formats, you'll definitely want to ask about strategic replacement plans. You'll also want to inquire about the library's ability to convert items from older formats to newer formats (say, from a filmstrip to a DVD) for both archival and accessibility purposes. Questions about how to navigate any copyright issues will also need to be resolved at this point. If your library is committed to maintaining the equipment to make these materials available long-term, you'll want to know who is responsible for troubleshooting if the equipment stops working. Finally, be sure you have a clear idea of how replacement and maintenance are funded. You may find that format replacement comes from your regular funds, in which case you'll want to plan spending very strategically as replacement items will compete with new purchases.

FORMAT UPDATES
Questions You Should Be Asking

- What older formats currently exist in my areas of collections responsibility?

- What types of equipment are available to handle these older formats?

- What are my options for changing formats?

- If I cannot buy the item in an updated format that works with current equipment, is there a way to preserve it or to convert the existing material into a new format? Will that process violate copyright?

- What are the costs of moving to a new format? Is there a special fund for that, or do I bear that burden myself?

- Is there any loss of quality by moving to a different format? If so, how reasonable is it to maintain the item in its current format?

- What should I do when I can't replace the item exactly? Are there guidelines for when that matters and when it doesn't?

Glossary

AACR2. *See Anglo-American Cataloguing Rules,* 2nd edition.

access points. Access points are the catalog record fields that are searchable in a catalog's public interface. These include authors, titles, and subject headings as well as numeric information such as the International Standard Book Number (ISBN).

acquisitions. The process by which a library purchases or acquires library resources, such as books, journals, or other materials. The term *acquisitions* may also refer to the library unit responsible for performing acquisitions functions for the library.

aggregated content. Information brought together in a single resource (a database, for example) from a variety of other sources. For example, aggregators may bring together—in one database—journals, magazines, and newspapers all produced by different publishers.

allocation. The amount of money provided to a liaison, department, or other entity for spending on library resources.

allocation formulas. Mathematical formulas used to determine allocations of funds. Usually multivariate, and variables may be weighted by importance.

Anglo-American Cataloging Rules, 2nd edition (AACR2). The cataloging code used in the United States and the English-speaking world from 1978 to 2013. The code provides for descriptions and creation of access points for most formats of library material. It was replaced by RDA, which was fully implemented by the Library of Congress in March 2013.

approval plan. An arrangement between a library and a vendor whereby the vendor automatically sends the library materials based on a preapproved profile.

authority control. The process of using one consistent form of a name, title, subject, or similar, in the library catalog and of referring alternate forms of these to the chosen or authorized form of the name.

A–Z list. An alphabetical list of databases and other resources provided by a library to its patrons. An A–Z list is typically publicly accessible.

batch. The workflow process by which materials are handled as a large group instead of as individual items. This process is often used for ordering items, receiving materials (particularly e-materials), and editing records.

bindery. Typically, an external company that provides hardcover binding of library materials, including paperback, spiral-bound, or damaged books.

collection designation. The concept that all physical items are designated to a specific collection (stacks, reference, etc.) within a library.

collection development. The acts and processes related to selecting and deselecting resources and maintaining collections. Collection development is strategic in nature, based on the library's mission, values, and patron community.

collection development policy. The formal documentation that sets forth collections guidelines.

collection level. The scope and depth at which a library aims to build its collection in any particular subject. The Library of Congress defines six levels of collection intensity: out-of-scope, minimal, basic information, instructional support, research, and comprehensive.

consortium. A group of libraries or institutions that work together for specific purposes. In this book, *consortium* generally refers to a group of libraries that work together to leverage greater buying power for library resources, particularly e-resources. Consortia may be formal, requiring membership dues and official agreements, or informal in nature.

contents note. A note in the catalog record of an item that provides additional descriptive information regarding the item's content. These are most often used for tables of contents.

continuing commitments. Resources that a library has committed to purchasing or leasing continuously; these commitments are usually multiyear in nature. Subscriptions are the most common continuing commitments for libraries. The counterpart to continuing commitments is one-time purchases.

controlled vocabulary. A scheme used to assign a particular word or phrase to represent a specific topic or idea. Controlled vocabularies are used for indexing and cataloging resources. Subject headings in catalog records employ controlled vocabularies.

copy cataloging. Creating records by using records that have already been created by another library or other cataloging agency. Copy cataloging includes record searching in specialized bibliographic databases and then modifying the record for local use by adding institution-specific information, such as bar codes and copy information.

database. In this book, *database* generally refers to an online product that provides access to indexes, abstracts, or the full text of resources.

DDA. *See* **demand-driven acquisitions.**

demand-driven acquisitions (DDA). Also known as patron-driven acquisitions, DDA is a method for acquiring library materials based on direct selection by library patrons. Typically, records for DDA items (most often e-books) are loaded into the catalog where they may be viewed or selected, or both, by patrons. DDA items do not require an expenditure of funds until they meet a predefined set of conditions based on actual use or access by patrons. These conditions, or "triggers," will vary by item and publisher.

discovery layer. A product that integrates access to various library resources into a single interface.

encumbrance. Funds that are reserved for items that have not yet been received by the library. In this book, encumbered funds generally apply to one-time purchases.

end-of-year (EOY) funds. Institutional funds that have not been spent or encumbered near the end of the fiscal year.

e-resources. Electronic resources of all types, including electronic versions of books, journals, magazines, and newspapers. *E-resources* can also refer to electronic versions of indexing and abstracting resources (e.g., databases), websites, digital collections, online data sets, and so forth.

expendables. Resources that are "used up" after a single use. A workbook is a good example of an expendable. Also sometimes referred to as consumables.

expenditure. Funds that have been disbursed to vendors for materials and resources received by the library.

full-time equivalent (FTE). Roughly, the population calculation intended to take into account individuals who are considered by the institution to be "part-timers" as well as those who are designated full time. *FTE* usually refers to either students or faculty and is generally used for reporting purposes.

FTE. *See* **full-time equivalent.**

headings. Access points within the online catalog. Examples of headings that are typically found in the catalog are subject headings, which create access based on topic, and name headings, which provide access to authors, editors, and others.

ILS. *See* **integrated library system.**

integrated library system (ILS). A software program used to manage or perform many functions within the library. Integrated library systems usually include components such as a public catalog interface, a circulation system, an acquisitions system, and so forth.

invoice. An itemized bill sent by vendors and publishers that includes a list of books or other purchased material.

invoicing. The process of providing payment for material included in an invoice. This is usually done through the integrated library system and will automatically update the internal accounts kept in the ILS.

jobber. A middleman or wholesaler who buys from publishers and other information resource producers and sells to libraries.

liaison. A librarian who has three main job responsibilities—reference and research, instruction, and collection development—for specific subject disciplines.

license. The agreement between a content provider and the library that specifies cost, access, content, and so forth. Licenses are considered to be legal documents.

link resolver. Software used to link library resources using URL information. Link resolvers are used when a full-text option is not initially available for a citation; information embedded in the citation's URL (volume, year, issue, etc.) is matched against other library resources to locate full-text options. Link resolvers often provide patrons with links to the full text, holdings information (particularly for physical materials), services such as interlibrary loan, or all of these.

Machine-Readable Cataloging (MARC). Standard for coding bibliographic information—for example, a catalog record—so that it can be read and transmitted by computer programs. MARC uses a three-digit numeric code to designate different parts of a record, with each field further subdivided into subfields.

MARC. *See* **Machine-Readable Cataloging.**

mediated approval. Approval by an intermediary group or individual *before* an item is submitted to acquisitions for purchase. New subscriptions or expensive one-time purchases are items that may require approval from both the liaison and another individual (e.g., collection development librarian) or group. Faculty-submitted orders may also undergo mediated approval by liaisons.

mediated ordering. Ordering that requires review by an acquisitions intermediary before purchase from a vendor. Often used to check for duplicates, collection policy disparity, and so forth.

metrics. In this book, *metrics* refers to categories of information (date, time, number of checkouts, last out date) used for both qualitative and quantitative measurement.

multiple-user purchase option (MUPO). A purchase option for electronic resources, usually e-books, that grants multiple users simultaneous access.

MUPO. *See* **multiple-user purchase option.**

notes field. A catalog record field that includes descriptive information useful to patrons or liaisons, such as table of contents information, and so on. Information entered into the notes field is generally accessible through keyword searches in the online catalog.

one-time purchases. Purchases of items that require funds only once and do not require ongoing allocations to pay for them. Monographs are the most common one-time purchases within libraries. The counterpart to one-time purchases is continuing commitments.

original cataloging. Creation of a new cataloging record from scratch instead of by using a record created by another library that matches the item-in-hand.

patron-driven acquisitions (PDA). *See* **demand-driven acquisitions (DDA).**

patron-initiated requests. Requests for materials that are initiated solely by the library's patrons rather than by librarians.

PDA. *See* **patron-driven acquisitions.**

pre-order searching. The search procedure performed after orders or item requests are submitted to acquisitions but before orders are placed with vendors. Often, pre-order searching is used to identify duplicate or dual-format requests.

processing. Typically refers to the actions used to physically prepare library materials for shelving. For books, these actions include stamping the books with the ownership stamp, adding security strips that work with the library's security system, adding date due slips, and affixing call numbers to the spine. *Processing* may also refer to the unit responsible for receiving items.

proxy server. A networked server with specialized software that allows library patrons to use e-resources remotely—that is, from locales other than the campus network. Patrons provide the proxy with information that verifies their institutional affiliation. After affiliation is verified, the proxy server changes the patron's remote IP address to one affiliated with the institution that will be recognized by the resource vendor, thus enabling access.

RDA. *See* ***Resource Description and Access.***

receiving. The concept of receiving items ordered by the library. *Receiving* may also refer to the unit responsible for receiving items or the process by which items are received.

reclassifying. The process of changing the classification of a resource. For physical items this involves changing the call number that is affixed to the item.

Resource Description and Access (RDA). The international cataloging code currently used by most libraries in the United States.

reversion. A budgetary situation wherein institutional units are required to return unspent but allocated funds (usually a certain percentage, but sometimes an actual amount) to the institution. Reversions are considered one-time situations, unlike budgetary cuts which are permanent.

rollover. In this book, rollovers are resource orders that roll over to the subsequent fiscal year when items are ordered but not received before the end of the fiscal year.

rush. The process of expediting requests. This process may apply to ordering, receiving and processing, or cataloging.

serials. Resources that are issued periodically and indefinitely. This term usually, but not always, refers to items such as scholarly journals, trade magazines, popular magazines, newspapers, and the like. It may also be used to refer to monograph series issued regularly and continually.

shelf-ready cataloging. A vendor-provided service whereby processing for library materials—such as stamping with ownership stamps, inserting security strips, and attaching spine labels—is done before the materials are sent to the library.

single-user purchase option (SUPO). A purchase option for electronic resources, usually e-books, that permits only one user to access that resource at any given time. Simultaneous access is not allowed.

standing orders. Generally used to refer to orders in which an item is issued in volumes or parts but is considered a single purchase and the library has agreed at the outset to purchase each volume or part as it is issued without having to order each volume or part separately. Items on standing orders may be issued regularly or irregularly, and payment amount may vary by volume or part (unlike a subscription).

subject headings. Fields in an item's catalog record that are used to describe the main subjects or topics of that item. Controlled vocabularies are most commonly used to create subject headings.

subscriptions. Agreements whereby a library purchases or leases content (e.g., journals, databases, etc.) that is issued continuously and is regularly scheduled. *Subscriptions* may also refer to the items received as part of a subscription agreement. Subscriptions are a type of continuing commitment.

SUPO. *See* **single-user purchase option.**

TAT. *See* **turnaround time.**

technical services. Broad term often used to describe non-public services units. In this book, *technical services* refers to the departments responsible for collection development, acquisitions, and cataloging.

turnaround time (TAT). Standard terminology that refers to the time it takes from initiation of a process to the completion of that same process.

turnaways. Phrase used to refer to the number of times an electronic resource *cannot* be accessed due to subscription or licensing restrictions.

vendor. Entity from whom the library purchases materials or access to resources, or both.

Bibliography

American Library Association, Reference and User Services Association. "Guidelines for Liaison Work in Managing Collections and Services." www.ala.org/rusa/resources/guidelines/guidelinesliaison.

Evans, G. Edward, and Margaret Zarnosky Saponaro. *Collection Management Basics.* 6th ed. Santa Barbara, CA: Libraries Unlimited, 2012.

Evans, G. Edward, Sheila S. Intner, and Jean Weihs. *Introduction to Technical Services.* 8th ed. Santa Barbara, CA: Libraries Unlimited, 2011.

Fales, Susan L., ed. *Guide for Training Collection Development.* Chicago: American Library Association, 1996.

Holden, Jesse. *Acquisitions in the New Information Universe: Core Competencies and Ethical Practices.* New York: Neal-Schuman, 2010.

Johnson, Peggy. *Fundamentals of Collection Development and Management.* 3rd ed. Chicago: ALA Editions, 2014.

Library of Congress, Cataloging and Acquisitions. "Collecting Levels." https://www.loc.gov/acq/devpol/cpc.html.

Macaluso, Stephen J., and Barbara Whitney Petruzzelli. "The Library Liaison Toolkit: Learning to Bridge the Communication Gap." *Reference Librarian* 89/90 (2005): 163–77.

Moniz, Richard, Jo Henry, and Joe Eshleman. *Fundamentals for the Academic Liaison.* Chicago: Neal-Schuman, 2014.

Stacy-Bates, Kristine K., et al. "Competencies for Bibliographers: A Process for Writing a Collection Development Competencies Document." *Reference and User Services Quarterly* 42, no. 3 (Spring 2003): 235–41.

Stoddart, Richard A., et al. "Going Boldly Beyond the Reference Desk: Practical Advice and Learning Plan for New Reference Librarians Performing Liaison Work." *Journal of Academic Librarianship* 32, no. 4 (July 2006): 419–27.

Tucker, James Cory, and Matt Torrence. "Collection Development for New Librarians: Advice from the Trenches." *Library Collections, Acquisitions and Technical Services* 28, no. 4 (Winter 2004): 397–409.

Weir, Ryan O., ed. *Managing Electronic Resources: A LITA Guide.* Chicago: ALA TechSource, 2012.

Wilkinson, Frances C., and Linda K. Lewis. *The Complete Guide to Acquisitions Management.* Westport, CT: Libraries Unlimited, 2003.

Index